Truth:
Fruit of Wisdom
and Love

Translated from the French
Original title : LA VERITE, FRUIT DE LA SAGESSE
ET DE L'AMOUR

Omraam Mikhaël Aïvanhov

Truth:
Fruit of Wisdom
and Love

Izvor Collection — No. 234

P R O S V E T A

Canadian Cataloguing in Publication Data

Aïvanhov, Omraam Mikhaël, 1900-1986

  Truth : fruit of wisdom and love

  (Izvor collection ; no. 234)
  Translation of: La vérité.
  ISBN 1-895978-03-3

   1. Truth. I. Title. II. Series: Izvor
  collection (Laval, Quebec) ; no. 234.

BJ1422.A4913 1994   121   C94-900260-7

       Prosveta S.A. — B.P. 12 — 83601 Fréjus Cedex (France)

Readers will better understand certain aspects of the lectures published in the present volume if they bear in mind that the Master Omraam Mikhaël Aïvanhov's teaching was exclusively oral and that the editors have made every effort to respect the flavor and style of each lecture.

The master's teaching is more than a body of doctrines:it is an organic whole,and his way of presenting it was to approach it from countless different points of view. By repeating certain aspects in a wide variety of contexts he constantly reveals a new dimension of the whole and, at the same time, throws new light on the individual aspects and on their vital links with each other.

TABLE OF CONTENTS

Chapter One

THE QUEST FOR TRUTH

In the ordinary course of our lives we often have occasion to say that something is true or not true and, depending on the circumstances, the word 'true' may not always mean quite the same thing. If we tell someone that what he says is not true we may mean that he is mistaken, or we may mean that he is lying. If he is mistaken it is usually because he does not know the truth. If he is lying, on the other hand, it means that he does know the truth and has some shady reason for wanting to conceal it.

Generally speaking we can say that truth, of which the contrary is error, belongs to the realm of science; whereas truth, of which the contrary is falsehood, belongs to the realm of morals or ethics. But people also commonly speak of their desire to discover the meaning of human destiny in general and their own life in particular as a quest for truth, and this kind of truth belongs to the realm of philosophy and religion. It is in this area that initiatic science can do so much to enlighten us and set us on the right path.

Many people are afraid to look the notion of truth in the face. They picture it as an ominous power that will take away their freedom to breathe, eat, drink and love. Try as you might to convince them that, on the contrary, truth will allow them to breathe and eat and love better than ever before, they remain unconvinced. Others speak of truth as something unattainable, as though it could only be found somewhere far, far away beyond the stars! But is it really so difficult to find the truth? Is it not rather that human beings do not know exactly what to look for or how to look for it? Or perhaps they like to think that it is difficult because this is a convenient excuse for their failings? In point of fact, it is not so difficult to find the truth if you look for it with sincerity. Is it possible to imagine that the Creator — or cosmic intelligence, or whatever you like to call it — should have made it impossible for man to find his way through life? We can accept the idea that the revelation of absolute truth can only be attained with difficulty; but it is totally unacceptable to suppose that man is incapable of finding the truth he needs in order to know where he is going and how to get there.

Many, many people have come and told me that they were seeking the truth. For years I would listen patiently to their tales, trying even to look impressed, for after all a man must be admired for devoting himself to the glorious quest for truth! And then, after many years, I began to be very irritated by all these people who take such pride in their search for the truth — and who never find it — and I decided to give some of them a lesson.

One day an elderly man said to me: 'I have been seeking the truth for more than fifty years!'

'Ah, and you have not found it?' I asked politely.

'No.'

'But you are still seeking?'

'Oh, yes,' he replied, with such an expression of smug self-satisfaction that it was obvious he was waiting for me to congratulate him on his perseverance. I looked at him for a long moment and then I said,

'My dear sir, let me tell you that you will never find it; the fact is that you are doing everything in your power not to find it!'

'How can you say that when I am seeking...'

'Yes, but you have already found the truth more than once in your lifetime. It is very easy to find the truth, for it is everywhere. You have often seen and heard and touched it, but you have never accepted it as truth, for you have always had so many other things in mind. You are looking for a "truth" to fit your own tastes, and when the truth you find does not suit you, you say: "No, no. That is not what I need," and you turn your back on it. You keep saying that you are seeking, but if we were to analyse exactly what it is you are seeking we would find that you are only seeking something that will allow you to satisfy your lusts and ambitions. No sir, forgive me for saying so, but you are not looking for the truth! You are looking for a servant to gratify all your whims. If you really wanted to find the truth you would have done so long ago. Even now you could find it if you wished, but that is not what you want.'

What a conversation! And I have had similar conversations with several different people... but I will not tell you what the outcome was.

It is enough for someone to say that he is a 'seeker after truth' for those around him to gaze at him in wonder and admiration. How wonderful actually to meet someone who is seeking the truth! Not having the slightest idea how to evaluate what he says, they are content to be impressed. Yes, it can be a profitable business this quest for truth. It can even be so materially rewarding that many people make a profession of it. They go from place to place lecturing about their fruitless search and write books about all their hopes and disappointments, and then, when their books are published, they receive all kinds of awards; receptions are given in their honour; they are regaled with snacks and sandwiches, cups of tea and glasses of champagne. A profitable business indeed!

Then there are those who start to seek the truth — as they think — because they realize that the energy and dynamism of their youth is beginning to desert them and they are forced to be less active. If you tell them that they will not find anything unless they are prepared to devote some time to reading, prayer, meditation and certain spiritual exercises, they say that they cannot spare the time, they are too busy. But they still say that they are 'seeking'! They have no lofty ideal in view and no notion that if they really want to find something they will have to start by changing many of the ideas they take for granted. In such conditions it is useless to seek the truth.

All human beings are looking for something, and each one gives that something a different name: happiness, the meaning of life, truth, and so on. Why do they not find what they are looking for? Because they always expect to find it in the form in which they picture it. Even truth is expected to conform to their idea of what it should be. And very often, when they decide to follow a spiritual teaching, it is in the hope of finding theories and situations that suit their preconceived notions. This is why so many people go from one teaching to another without ever settling down. There is always something that does not suit them: they do not like the look of their fellow-disciples; they were not given a sufficiently cordial reception; they cannot see any material advantage to be gained; the teaching demands too much of them; the master does not promise to fulfil all their dreams, and so on and so forth.

People are looking for lies, illusions, soap bubbles; and because a genuine master refuses to peddle illusions they turn away from him. They are unhappy in his school or they feel as though they were being coerced, and this is a sure sign that they are not really looking for the truth. Truth does not coerce people or make them miserable; if that is how they feel it is because truth is not what they are really looking for. If it were they would be happy.

No, although they continue to declare that they are seeking the truth they do not really want to find it. They wear their self-bestowed title as 'a seeker after truth' in their buttonholes as though it were a medal of honour! Well it is high time they changed this particular medal and put in its place one that says, 'I have found the right path and now I am hard at work'! But this does not suit them at all; they prefer to continue as before, wilful and exacting, expecting God himself to defer to their wishes. But however demanding and importunate they may be today, the time will come when they are obliged to acknowledge that none of their expectations are being realized. The fact is that the divine world cannot be forced. Truth reveals itself only to those who have the right attitude.

People look for truth in the same way that for centuries men looked for wives. What they were really looking for was a servant to give them children, cook and do the housework for them, wash and mend their clothes and put up with their bad temper. Yes, but there is no servant whose name is truth. It is the other way round: truth is a princess and man must be her servant, her gallant knight. Do you want to be her prince consort? Why not? There is no law against it. The only condition is that you must show yourself to be worthy of the honour by rising to her level and not trying to drag her down to yours. The psychic world is governed by the same laws as the physical world. Any Tom, Dick or Harry cannot expect to walk into the royal palace, declaring that he is going to

marry the princess and be proclaimed heir to
the throne. All the fairy-tales you heard in your
youth taught you that every young upstart who
asked the king for his daughter's hand in
marriage had to submit to certain ordeals, and
if he failed to pass the test he had to die. Well,
you should think about the lesson of these
fairy-tales for it applies equally to truth. Truth
is the daughter of God, and if you ask for her
hand without being ready to serve her and show
her that you are worthy of the honour, you will
simply be demonstrating your monstrous pride
and she will send you packing. Truth is the
daughter of a king and she is just as
uncompromising as a fairy-tale princess. She
will never lower herself or bow to your will,
and if you refuse to serve her not only will you
fail to win her hand but you will die spiritually.
Perhaps you will say that truth is cruel; yes and
no. It all depends on your attitude.

You will never find truth unless you make
up your mind to serve her. Even many very
spiritual people will never find truth because
they expect her to help them to achieve their
most material ambitions. As I say, they look on
truth as a servant, or perhaps as a bank account
that can give them material possessions, power,
the means to seduce women, and so on. No,
truth is a princess, and if she sees that you want
her to stoop to do all kinds of humiliating jobs

for you, she will simply dismiss you with scorn and indignation. Unfortunately, the theories that young people learn at home and in their schools have created a mentality in society at large which reinforces this attitude of selfishness and insensitivity. The world is full of people who constantly clamour for what they want and try to impose their will on others, without the slightest suspicion that it is precisely their violence and disrespect that closes all doors to them.

If you want to find the truth you must be humble. And to be humble means first of all to stop being so greedy in your attitude toward nature, your fellow human beings and your Creator. 'That is all very well, but we have so many needs.' Very well, let us take a closer look at some of those needs. Who is it exactly who is always asking for something? Who is it who demands ease, comfort and pleasure? Who is it who refuses all efforts, constraints or obligations? It is your lower nature. And is your lower nature really you? No, it is not.

Our lower nature is part of us but it is not our true self. It is the raw material that we have to work with in order to nourish our immortal, eternal higher nature. It is with our higher nature that we must identify. As long as people make the mistake of identifying with their lower nature they will believe that it is they who want this, that or the other thing; that it is they who have been hurt or insulted; that it is they who are suffering. They will continue to go through life saying that they are searching and searching for the truth without ever finding it. If you want to find the truth you must identify with the light, nobility and integrity of your higher nature.

Chapter Two

TRUTH,

THE CHILD OF WISDOM AND LOVE

Many people have a strange way of talking about how they expect to find truth. They seem to think that they will meet someone one day who will say, 'Behold, my name is Truth. You have found me at last. Now, listen carefully and I will tell you exactly what to think and what to do...' But, of course, this is not at all how it happens.

If you want to understand this question of finding truth you must begin by studying man's psychic anatomy. Our psyche is built on a triple foundation: the intellect, which enables us to think; the heart, which enables us to feel emotions, and the will, which enables us to act. The will never does anything on its own initiative; it always needs to be set in motion by thoughts and feelings.

Observe yourselves and you will see that your will is set in motion or not depending on what you think and feel about people and things. The thought that work is a useful activity, for instance, is not sufficient to make you decide to work; you also need to like work. Or if you come across a wounded man by the roadside, the thought that he needs your help is not enough to make you decide to do something about it; you also need to feel some sympathy for him. And if a man attacks his neighbour and tries to knock him out, you can be sure that it is not only because he has made up his mind that the man is stupid or wicked; his action has to be triggered by a feeling of hatred, exasperation, or anger. And so on... I could give you any number of examples, but the point is that our daily lives are made up of actions inspired by both thoughts and feelings. The proportion in which the two factors intervene varies but both of them are always present.

It would be true to say therefore that our actions bear witness not only to the existence, but also to the nature of the thoughts in our minds and the feelings in our hearts; they are the offspring of those thoughts and feelings, and, depending on whether the 'parents' are good or evil, our actions will themselves be good or evil. They will be good only if the intellect is inspired by wisdom and the heart by love. The ideal of the intellect is to manifest wisdom; the ideal of the heart is to manifest love, and the ideal of the resulting act of the will is to manifest truth. This means that insofar as the thoughts of your intellect strive for wisdom and the feelings of your heart strive for love, you abide in truth. And there you have the whole secret of truth. It is very simple.

Truth has been defined in so many different ways that the whole question has become hopelessly involved. The fact is that one cannot define truth, for it does not exist as such. Only wisdom and love exist. It is easy to say that you have found the truth. A great many people make this claim, but when you see how they behave it is only too obvious that the truth they claim to have found is not inspired by wisdom and love. It is a person's behaviour that shows whether he or she is living in truth, not the theories or fantasies they may talk about. The extraordinary thing is that human beings have made truth into a kind of abstraction, whereas, on the contrary, it is in the way they behave and live their daily lives that it can be seen as a concrete reality.

You must never again say that you are looking for the truth or that you have failed to find it, for there is nothing to look for and nothing to be found. There is only one thing to do and that is to grow in wisdom and love. And you must also stop saying that you abide in truth. There is no claim to be made in this respect: if you possess love and wisdom you also possess truth, whether you lay claim to it or not, and everyone will be able to sense this. Perhaps the comparison will surprise you, but I like to think of truth as a medal or coin, one face of which is love and the other wisdom. You will never find truth as an isolated element, for it cannot be conceived independently of the heart and the mind. It is your love and wisdom that will show you truth.

If there are so many different and contradictory 'truths' in circulation in the world today, it is because they reflect the deformities of heart and mind of today's human beings. When someone says, 'For me the truth is thus and so,' he is talking only about his own truth, and that truth expresses his own heart and mind, which may be distorted or simply inadequate, or which may be very highly developed. If truth were independent of the activities of our hearts and minds we should all have discovered the same truth. But this is not the case, as you very well know: we all discover different truths. All, that is, except those who possess true love and true wisdom. Such beings have all discovered the same truth; this is why they speak the same language.

Everything depends, therefore, on the harmonious development of heart and mind, and, on a higher plane, of soul and spirit. Those who are not vigilant drift away from the truth and if they then write books to put forward their erroneous point of view they lead others astray also. It is not that they are insincere; they are sincere, but they are in error. Sincerity and truth are not the same thing. You can be sincere even if your understanding is totally erroneous; you must not try to justify your error on the grounds that you are sincere.

As I have said, people make the mistake of thinking of truth as an abstraction; this is why the whole question is so obscure. But truth is the world in which we live; we are inseparably bound to it, one with it, we cannot be cut off from it. We live in truth, we eat and breathe truth, and it is time we stopped thinking of it as something external to our being. The men and women we meet in life and the objects we use — books, works of art, and so on — are all external, and they can do no more than awaken within us an intuition of the truth. This is why I say that to go in search of the truth is the surest way of never finding it. Truth is not something that you can find on this earth, and you are deluding yourself if you hope to come across something external one day of which you can say, 'Here is the truth!' The only way to come closer to truth is to understand and manifest love and wisdom.

Now, if you have understood what I have been saying, you will feel the need to analyse yourselves. What are your feelings? Are they truly inspired by love? And what about your thoughts? Are they in keeping with wisdom? Is there no element in them that might lead you into error? Each time you inject an element of love or wisdom into your feelings or your thoughts you are achieving truth; you are making contact with a certain aspect, achieving a certain degree or level of truth, and these aspects and degrees are infinite in number. Truth must be grasped and sought at the same time. In other words, we must grasp and cling to the two irrefutable principles of love and wisdom, and at the same time we must continue to seek the most perfect forms in which to express them.

Chapter Three

WISDOM AND LOVE;

LIGHT AND WARMTH

The union of wisdom and love gives birth to truth, to life of a fuller, more intense nature. And as this life floods into you it waters the seeds buried in your soul and stimulates the growth of an abundance of flowers and fruit, that is to say, an abundance of luminous thoughts and warm feelings.

Wisdom represents the masculine principle and love the feminine principle, and each is naturally drawn to the other, whereas wisdom repulses wisdom and love repulses love. It is important to take this into consideration in human relationships. A great many marriages break up because both partners are either too reserved or too impassioned. A relationship is more likely to stand the test of time if the temperaments of those concerned are different and complementary.

On the physical plane, light and heat are the
symbols of wisdom and love, with which they
have many points in common: wisdom
resembles light, in that it can focus on
infinitesimal details; heat resembles love in its
capacity to expand and embrace vast horizons.
When you first meet someone about whom you
know absolutely nothing you have no reason to
love him. It is your intellect that comes into
play and takes note of what it sees: the colour
of his eyes, the shape of his nose and mouth,
his gestures and mannerisms, his profession,
his income, and so forth. But when you meet
someone you love you are not interested in
analysing these details, you accept him just as
he is; your vibrations are in unison with his
because it is the whole person you love. Even if
he does something reprehensible you forgive
him for it; his faults are details that your love
ignores. As soon as you stop loving him,
however, you notice and dissect and criticize
every little fault.

Let me give you an example. Suppose a
chemist or biologist is in his laboratory
working on a few molecules of gas or a
microscopic sample of plant or animal tissue.
All his attention is focused on these minute
particles of matter. But this distinguished
scientist is in love. When he leaves his
laboratory in the evening all his thoughts are

with his beloved, and the starry sky over his head seems too narrow to contain his love. The flowers in the parks and gardens he passes seem to be only a poor expression of the graces and virtues he sees in her and he longs to give her all the palaces and all the treasures on earth. Then one day his romance begins to turn sour, his ardour cools and his darling's charms suddenly seem less endearing. He begins to notice and find fault with every little thing that is not to his liking: 'You're late, you haven't washed my shirt, you've lost my cuff-links again, you have put too much salt in the soup, you forgot to buy a newspaper...' Every insignificant detail is magnified out of all proportion, as though he were looking at it through the lens of his high-powered microscope.

The warmth that filled his heart has been replaced by the light that shows up every little detail. Yes, but what is the nature of this light? It is certainly not spiritual. It is the ordinary light that is associated with electricity. When we sense that a quarrel is about to erupt between two people we say that there is electricity in the air. Electricity can be used to produce light, but it is not in itself light.

Just as electricity is associated with light, magnetism is associated with heat. Heat dilates and magnetism attracts; both are manifested by

an expansion or flowering, an enhancement of
volume or form. This is true on the physical
plane and it is also true on the psychic plane.
People are said to be warm or magnetic when
they have a kind of inner spaciousness which
others find very attractive. Light and electricity,
however, produce the opposite effect. People
are not attracted by those who possess light,
knowledge, because it makes them feel inferior
and they are afraid of being judged; they prefer
to keep their distance. And, of course, someone
who is too highly charged with electricity
actually repulses others.

Now, it is up to you to understand how and
when to use love (warmth and magnetism) and
wisdom (light and electricity). Love binds and
wisdom loosens. Wisdom enables you to
distinguish good from evil; it also enables you
to repulse evil. But even your friends will not
be comfortable with you if you use only
wisdom. Wisdom is luminous, to be sure, but it
is cold, and people are not particularly fond of
the cold, even if it is luminous. This explains
why those who are wise are often rather solitary
beings, whereas those who are warm but less
wise are often surrounded by friends. So what
is the answer? Should you avoid solitude by
forgetting about wisdom? No, of course not, for
that would only lead to the danger of being
invaded and having your hands tied by too

many attachments. The great difficulty is to learn how to get the two currents to flow harmoniously within you; to learn when to manifest love and when to manifest wisdom.

I have already explained how water solves this problem by constantly rising and falling between the heavens and the earth.[1] It rises in order to develop wisdom and falls in order to manifest love. It rises to receive the blessings of heaven and falls to pass on these blessings to the earth. To take and to give, receive and pass on: this is truth; this is the accomplishment of God's will.

Our Father which art in heaven,
Hallowed be thy name.
Thy kingdom come.
Thy will be done
In earth as it is in heaven.

In these first three lines of the Lord's Prayer we find an application of what I have been explaining about wisdom, love and truth.

Hallowed be thy name: to bless or hallow something belongs to the sphere of wisdom, of light. It is light that blesses and illuminates the works of God. If our understanding is properly

---

1 See *The Mysteries of Fire and Water*, Izvor Collection, No. 232, Chap. 11.

illuminated we bless everything we touch. Why
should we bless God's name? Because a name
is the sum and synthesis of all the constituent
elements. The name of God comprehends and
contains all forms and all living beings.

Thy kingdom come: the kingdom of God,
the reign of God, is the reign of perfect love.
There can be no kingdom if there is no love, for
love is the cement that binds the parts into a
whole. Without love a kingdom falls apart.
Love as understood by an initiate is not a
passing sentiment but a stable, constant state of
consciousness in which one is in harmony with
the whole of creation.

Thy will be done: those who, through
wisdom and love, bless the name of God and
establish his reign within their own being are
necessarily doing his will. To do the will of
God is to possess truth, to dwell in truth.

All Christians recite this prayer; indeed it is
the one they recite most often, but it does not
follow that they always understand its deepest
meaning. But now, thanks to what I have just
told you, you can say the Lord's Prayer and be
conscious of what you are saying.

In fact, here is an exercise you can do. Sit
quietly with your hands on your knees. Breathe
in to the count of six while saying inwardly,
'Lord, may thy name be hallowed within me.'
Hold your breath to the count of six while

saying, 'May thy kingdom come within me.' Breathe out to the count of six, saying, 'May thy will be done through me.' If you do this exercise four or five times a day for several weeks, you will feel that something within you has expanded and become more luminous and more serene. For twenty centuries thousands and millions of Christians have recited this prayer, and although they may not always have been fully conscious of what they were doing, their work has made of these words a living formula, a reservoir of invisible forces. Today, when you say them consciously, you are tapping this great reservoir and drawing on its beneficial forces to help you to continue and improve your work.

Meditate on wisdom, which is concerned with little things, and on love, which is concerned with bigger things. Wisdom affects only a few minute particles of our being; it has never been known to produce a major upheaval in anyone's life. Love, on the other hand, can transform a person's behaviour instantaneously; sometimes it can even transform their physical appearance. The greatest transformations can only be achieved by love, not by wisdom. Wisdom is there to guide us, but love is the operative factor.

Chapter Four

THE LOVE OF A DISCIPLE;

THE WISDOM OF A MASTER

Solitude usually provides the best conditions for the acquisition of knowledge. Mental activities such as reading, reflection and meditation do not generally require the presence or participation of other people. In fact other people are often more hindrance than help. On the other hand, the presence of others incites us to draw on our knowledge in order to share it with them; it is their presence that awakens our desire to communicate.

A desire to communicate knowledge, however, can only be fulfilled if those destined to receive this knowledge are attentive and receptive. This is a necessary condition: that they trust the person who is able to instruct them. Teachers and professors who are willing to share their knowledge are so often chilled and paralysed by the attitude of their pupils and students. Critical remarks or a lack of attention may not deter teachers from giving their

lectures, but they effectively kill any desire they
might have to explore their subject in depth
with their students and to give the best of
themselves. On the other hand, a teacher may
come to his class-room after a sleepless night
feeling tired and worried and not at all in the
mood to give his lesson, but if he finds his
pupils open and receptive, he will immediately
feel revived, stimulated and inspired.

This is something that all teachers and
lecturers — also all spiritual masters — have
experienced. However ready and willing an
instructor may be, he can never satisfy more
than fifty per cent of the conditions required for
the transmission of knowledge. It is up to his
disciples or students to provide the other fifty
per cent by their receptive, sympathetic
attitude.

Once again this brings us back to the role of
heart and intellect. The heart is the disciple
who is open to the knowledge that the
instructor, the intellect, offers him; it is the
ante-room of the intellect. The heart prepares
the intellect and gets it into a good mood before
bringing us into its presence, just as a servant
ushers a guest into the presence of his master.
We have to win the friendship of the heart
therefore in order to gain entry to the intellect.
When you want an appointment with somebody
important you have to be introduced by his

secretary. Similarly, if you want to gain entry to wisdom you have to be introduced by love. The only way to gain entry to the great mysteries is to open one's heart.

The intellect does not like to be kissed and caressed. It prefers discussion, debate, the shock of ideas, because it is these that force it to develop. If you want your intellect to work you must not warm it, that will only put it to sleep; you must keep it cool, that is to say, you must keep it on the qui vive by surprising it and giving it obstacles to overcome. Difficulties and ordeals are useful because they unsettle you and force you to react and to reflect, and in this way they teach you wisdom. Agreeable circumstances, on the other hand, influence the heart towards greater generosity, warmth and love, for when something is warm it has a tendency to expand and unfold. It is important to have an attitude of openness and receptivity and it is the heart that makes this possible. So, as I say, we have to win the consent of the heart in order to have access to the intellect; we have to possess love in order to acquire wisdom. Wisdom can only be acquired through love.

When a master reveals to his disciples the reality of the spiritual world, with all its treasures and all its mysteries, he is giving them something that he has to wrench from his own soul, his own life, and if he senses that his audience is not ready or has no real interest, no respect or reverence for the knowledge he is ready to give them, something within him closes up.

A disciple's love must unite with his master's wisdom, and it is the union of that love and wisdom that gives birth to truth. A master does not need your wisdom — which, in any case, you would be incapable of giving him — but he does need your love. His role is not to love you but to enlighten you; it is up to you to give him your trust and love, for this is the best way to be sure of receiving his wisdom. It is very simple: a disciple loves his master and the master enlightens his disciple. If you try to reverse this order of things you will remain in darkness for a very long time.

Perhaps you will object that when people speak of spiritual masters they always stress that they are great lovers of mankind. Yes, this is certainly true, for to want to help and enlighten others one has to love them. But the nature of a master's love is different. It is a love illuminated by wisdom, and this is something that a disciple often fails to understand; he always wants his master to smile and say nice things to him. If a disciple thinks that his master does not love him he may feel unhappy and rebellious because he does not realize that if his master sometimes treats him severely and gives him a good shaking up it is for his own good. It is important to understand that a master's love must always be accompanied by a certain severity.

To meet a genuine master and become his disciple is one of the greatest blessings life has to offer, but only on condition that you receive this blessing with the right attitude and are capable of loving him, for a disciple's love influences his master. I assure you, this is so! All creatures are linked to each other and influence each other. A master influences his disciples but a disciple also influences his master. The sincere, selfless love of a disciple causes his master's love to grow.

Every teacher, in whatever kind of school, finds it easier to teach those of his students who are eager to learn. He will try to help all of them, of course, but he will be far more inspired and stimulated by those who are attentive and anxious to learn. The law of reciprocity applies on every level: love gives birth to wisdom and wisdom inspires love. The two are necessary in order to attain truth.

Chapter Five

TRUTH, THE KERNEL OF LIFE

If you want to see how nature works you only need to study a fruit. All fruits have an outer sheath which, depending on whether it is thick or thin, soft or hard, is known as the skin, shell, peel or husk. Sometimes this outer sheath is fit for human consumption but more often than not we throw it away and eat only the flesh which is inside. Inside that again is the kernel or seeds which are also usually thrown away but which, if planted, reproduce the species. A fruit, therefore, is built on the same pattern as a cell, for a cell consists of a membrane, which is like a little pocket that surrounds and contains the liquid matter known as the cytoplasm, and in the centre of the cytoplasm is the kernel or nucleus.

Wherever you look in nature — in man, in the family, in society or in the universe as a whole — you will see this same pattern of three elements. Both the infinitely great and the infinitesimally small are built on the model of the cell. Symbolically, the membrane corresponds to the physical plane, the cytoplasm to the astral plane of feelings and the nucleus to the mental plane of thought.

And now let us get back to the fruit and see how we can interpret these three elements, skin, flesh and kernel. The skin, which envelopes and protects the fruit, corresponds to the physical plane; the flesh, in which flow the currents of life, corresponds to the psychic plane, and the kernel, which ensures the reproduction of the fruit, corresponds to the spiritual plane. And what do these three elements represent in the spiritual life? The skin of a fruit represents wisdom, which protects, contains and preserves; the flesh is love, for love is the nourishment that sustains life, and the kernel that is planted represents truth, for only what is true can perpetuate life.

Suppose I give you a fruit. Can you truthfully say that you know what it is? No, you cannot know it in its entirety unless you know its three elements. What should a disciple do with a fruit? Once he has peeled it and eaten the flesh, he must plant the kernel or seeds; only in this way can he hope to know the truth.

If you ask an initiate to reveal truth to you he will not give you all kinds of complicated, abstract explanations. He will offer you a fruit and tell you to eat it. And when you have eaten it, what will you do with the kernel? Will you throw it away? Remember that it is the kernel that contains the truth! The whole fruit, the whole tree in fact, is contained in the seed, and if you want to know its secrets you have to plant that seed in the ground and wait. While you are waiting you will have time to see how the sun and rain work to make it grow and produce a stem and leaves and branches. From that one kernel will emerge a great tree, and only when that tree is fully grown will you know the truth that lay hidden in the kernel.

Most human beings know only the skin, the husk of life. Some try to taste the inner content, but even that is not enough; you also have to plant the kernel and wait to see what it produces. In other words, you must look upon all that happens to you as though it were a fruit which has been handed to you: ask yourself which part should be thrown away, which part you should eat, and which part should be planted. Once you are capable of doing these three things correctly you will never commit any more blunders.

Let me give you an example. Suppose a man or woman tells you every day how much they love you: if you swallow their words whole without sorting the edible from the inedible, you will soon find yourself in deep trouble. Why? Because you have not learned the lesson contained in a fruit. Certainly, the love and the words that express it contain many good and beautiful elements, and you would be right to eat them. But you must realize that, coming as they do from a human being, both the love and its expression are necessarily mixed with other elements that are all too human. You must leave those other elements on the side of your plate.

Love is a very complex question. If someone offers you their love you must realize that in that love there will always be elements that you will have to discard, others that you can accept, and one that you must plant in your soul. If you are wise you will tell the person who offers you love, 'Wait a little. Before answering you I must plant the kernel. The fruit is very sweet and juicy, but I want to know what kind of tree it will produce.' Once you know the nature of that love you can make up your mind without endangering the future.

Take another example. Suppose a business man offers you a partnership and assures you that in no time at all your fortune will be made and you will become a person of influence. You are so dazzled by the promise of a brilliant future that you swallow the offer whole — skin, flesh and kernel. In other words you commit yourself all the way. For a time you eat all you can, but then you begin to have heartburn and nausea (by which I mean that deals fall through, you lose money, you are on the verge of bankruptcy, and so on) and the doctor (divine wisdom) prescribes a strong purge. What brought you to such a pass? Your own ignorance. All the wonderful things you were offered contained something poisonous. You should have begun by planting the seed to see what the end product would be.

Life constantly faces us with this question: what kind of tree is lying dormant in the kernel that is being offered to us? What will be its fruits? Always ask yourself this before swallowing anything whole. Remember the words of Hermes Trismegistus: 'You shall separate the fine from the coarse with great diligence.' True, this precept applies primarily to alchemical operations, but not exclusively; it is applicable to every area of life. In everything we see and hear and touch there is always something to discard, something to accept and something to plant. You should even apply this rule to what I tell you in my lectures, for there are always some elements that are too indigestible for you, and that you should leave to one side, others that you can eat and yet others that you must plant. Practically speaking therefore you should concentrate on the elements that you understand and look for the kernel they contain so that you may plant it.

Some of you may say, 'What is all this talk about planting and sowing? I have not got a garden. Where am I supposed to plant things?' What about your brain? The brain is a field, an excellent seed-bed. What do you think a master does? He sows seeds in the brains of his disciples. Sometimes, of course, his disciples are unhappy because they do not understand what he is doing, but the master tells them, 'Be patient! These seeds will soon produce a tree and then you will be happy to have its fruit to refresh you and satisfy your hunger.'

Chapter Six

'I AM THE WAY, THE TRUTH,
AND THE LIFE.'

And the Lord God planted a garden eastward in Eden; and there he put the man whom he had formed.

And out of the ground made the Lord God to grow every tree that is pleasant to the sight, and good for food; the tree of life also in the midst of the garden, and the tree of knowledge of good and evil.

And a river went out of Eden to water the garden; and from thence it was parted and became into four heads.[1]

Reading this passage from the Book of Genesis you will perhaps be puzzled by the reference to the four branches of the river, and you will wonder what they correspond to. They correspond to the four currents that divide the

---

1 Genesis 2, 8-10.

universe, and they have great magical significance. It is from them that come what we know as the four points of the compass.

A river, with all its tributaries and branches, symbolizes the currents of life. Space is criss-crossed by multiple currents of forces and energies, and our own bodies are irrigated by arteries, veins and capillaries which correspond to the rivers and streams that irrigate the earth. The river that you see flowing through your own little bit of town or countryside is not really adequate to help you to understand the importance of this symbol. You must also think about where that river comes from and where it is going. In other words, you must think of its source and its outlet.

Jesus revealed the full spiritual dimension of the symbol of the river when he said, 'I am the way, the truth and the life.' Perhaps you see no connection between these words and the image of a river, but to an initiate the connection is clear; when he hears these words he immediately pictures a river flowing down from the mountain. 'The way' is the river bed, the channel; 'life' is the water flowing along that channel, and 'truth' is the spring from which flows that life.

And now let me carry the interpretation one step further. What is this 'way' which provides a channel for life and which we can follow upstream to the source? It is wisdom. And life, that is to say, the water that washes over stones, irrigates plants and quenches the thirst of men and beasts... this water is love. So in effect Jesus was saying, 'I am the path of wisdom; I am the love that gives birth to divine life; I am the source of truth from which flows this life.' Water always symbolizes life and love. The vital energies and forces that flow through nature are represented as water, a fluid that irrigates, quenches thirst and sustains life.

This image of a spring and of the river that flows from it, therefore, corresponds to a reality of the spiritual life. It contains also the essence of our teaching, which is based on love (water), wisdom (the river bed) and truth (the spring or source).

The symbolism of a river can be applied to every aspect of life. Those who wish to turn back to the source, to truth, must follow the path of wisdom. If the source dries up there will be no more water in the river, but at least the channel remains as evidence of what was. It is a vestige, and as such it has something to teach us; it belongs to the realm of wisdom. Of course, in this context we must understand the word wisdom in a very broad sense. Just as the river bed endures, so does wisdom endure, for it is a form, and forms are material; they endure on the physical plane as relics, monuments, books, and so on. Even if love and life have vanished the form still remains. Many houses stand empty, abandoned long ago by those who lived in them, but they are still there. Rocks and mountains are still there, also, even if their soul has left them. All that endures corresponds to the realm of wisdom. Wisdom will endure for all eternity in order to bear witness to what was and what will be.

Those who want to learn can always do so by consulting wisdom, for wisdom survives every cataclysm; its mark is etched into everything that exists. Every object, even the smallest vestige of the past, necessarily bears the mark and seal of wisdom. Archeologists try to reconstruct the history of mankind by collating a few scattered remnants such as bones, fragments of flint or earthenware, and when they are successful their work is very instructive. There is much to be learned and to be reflected upon in what they discover.

Unlike wisdom, which is stable, love is mobile, always on the move. It refuses to be poured into a mould or bound to one form. Love is a living, moving being; you cannot pin it down or expect to find it always in the same place. All you can do is follow the trace of its footprints and see where it once dwelt. You meet someone of the opposite sex and for a few minutes, while you are together, something about that person — their expression, their smile, the way they look at you — sends you into raptures; you feel as though you were in heaven. A week later — or the very next day perhaps — you meet the same person and to your astonishment you feel nothing special. The love you had glimpsed has moved on; it is no longer there.

Love is an essence which is far too subtle to be locked up, but wisdom is always there, unchanging; it is always available to you if you are capable of deciphering the messages it leaves behind. You will object that all those old forms have been burned; that there is nothing left but a handful of ashes. Yes, but in spite of that, wisdom is still there. Those ashes make it possible for you to reconstruct the whole story.

Love is a living being; it does not dwell in tombs or ruins. You say that there is still life to be found in tombs and ruins. Yes, the life of snakes, scorpions and bats, and all kinds of plant life. But that is not the life I am talking about. I am talking about the life that dwells only in that subtlest and most refined of vessels, love.

Love is the water that flows from the spring of truth. This means that if truth is absent there can be no love. In order to find truth we have to follow the path of wisdom, but in order to drink that truth and live in it we must have love. It is possible to reach the spring of truth simply by following the path of wisdom, but if you have only wisdom you will not be able to drink from it. If you have love, on the other hand, you do not need wisdom in order to drink at the spring of truth.

Many philosophers and scientists say that they have found truth, but you only have to look at them to see that they are dried up, and this is a sure sign that they have not really found truth. Outwardly, perhaps, by following the path of wisdom, they have found the source, but their own inner spring has run dry and this shows that they do not really possess truth. Those who possess truth come to it more by love than by wisdom. Wisdom enables you to find truth but only love enables you to possess it as a living reality within you. Nature itself teaches us this important distinction.

None of this is my own invention; I am only explaining to you what I find in the great book of nature. If you want to work with wisdom you can do so without moving a limb; you can spend your life with a book in a library. But if you want to work with love you are going to have to go out and about in order to meet your sweetheart, to see the sun and the flowers, to listen to the song of birds, to help those who are in need, to buy a loaf of bread. Love forces you to move about because it is always on the move; it is as mobile as water, and those who want to find it have to hurry to catch up, otherwise it will be gone again.

The story of mankind can be compared to the story of the earth itself. Love, like water, is constantly moving. Water may cover a whole continent for thousands of years, and as it draws back into lakes and rivers, dry land appears which is soon covered with vegetation. Where there is a good supply of water, that is to say, where love is abundant, new cultures are born, for the spirits of light always work where love is to be found. When water disappears completely the land dries up and dies, but the vestiges of wisdom will still be there for archeologists to study. This is the case of the Sahara.

In the proximity of great rivers there is always an abundance of love, that is to say, rich cultures and civilizations. If you want luminous spirits to come and work within you, you must take care not to be dry. If you are dry they will not come to you. And if you protest that you are very wise, I can only say that that may be so, but you are a vestige of the past. Nothing grows in your soil any more. The best one can say about you is that once upon a time there was a flourishing civilization, an important initiatic centre on this spot, but that it has all disappeared, buried by the sand.

It is all very well to make a pilgrimage to venerate the tomb of Christ, but this does not mean very much, for Christ is no longer there. The river has changed its course; it flows elsewhere, wherever there is love. Many people can tell us a great deal about civilizations that have disappeared, and it is all very interesting, but it is not what really matters. What matters is the life that is flowing today. In any case, think of all the Christians who have gone to look for traces of Jesus' life in Palestine: how many of them would be his followers if he were to come back today? Not only would most of them fail to recognize him, they would persecute him and clamour for his death.

It is easy to walk along a dried-up river bed. It is more difficult to embrace the infinite richness of water that is alive and constantly new, but you must always seek what is alive. You will never find truth amongst the dead. If you base your life on values that have disappeared you too will disintegrate and fall into ruin. It is your own choice that determines your destiny. From the point of view of magic, it is always dangerous to cling to something that has disintegrated or disappeared. If you want to seek truth by following the path of wisdom, by all means do so, but be sure to drink the living water as well. Cling to that which renews itself every day, to that which rises, to that which is eternally fresh and new because it continues to grow. This is why I tell you to keep an image of the sun always alive within you. Do not worry if you have read somewhere that even the sun is destined to die one day; in the meantime make it the central symbol of your spiritual life.

Build your houses with the solid materials of wisdom if you want to, but be sure that a living soul dwells within them, for otherwise you will soon see signs of decay on the walls. A house that is lived in deteriorates less rapidly than one that is empty, for the living, breathing presence of human beings gives it life. It is as though the house resolved to keep in good shape for the sake of those who have found shelter within its walls. When it is abandoned it begins to disintegrate. This is always the way. So build your house on a framework of wisdom, but consolidate it and make sure that it endures by filling it with love. If there is no life in it, it will collapse. This is what we witness when a man's soul leaves his body: the body immediately begins to decompose. What had kept it standing before? The life that flowed within. And now there is nothing but a corpse. What is the truth of a corpse?

Perhaps you are now beginning to understand the profound meaning of these words: 'I am the way, the truth and the life.'

Christ himself is telling us, 'I am the life (love) that flows in the river; I am the path (wisdom) that you can follow to work your way up to the source (truth). Come to this river every day in thought; drink this water that flows from on high; slake your thirst at the pure, transparent source of love. When you possess love every heavenly blessing is yours and the waters of true life flow through you.'

Chapter Seven

THE BLUE RAY OF TRUTH

In answer to Pilate's interrogation Jesus said: 'To this end was I born, and for this cause came I into the world, that I should bear witness to the truth. Everyone that is of the truth hears my voice.'

But when Pilate asked, 'What is truth?' Jesus did not reply. You will soon begin to see why not.

Before this, in his last encounter with his disciples, Jesus had said: 'I have yet many things to say unto you, but ye cannot bear them now. Howbeit when he the Spirit of truth is come, he will guide you into all truth.'

Many people hope that one day they will meet an initiate who will reveal truth to them. They picture a spectacular scene in which lightning and thunder flash and roar, the walls tremble and a supernatural voice speaks to them. They see themselves transformed in the twinkling of an eye, their feet firmly set on the path of righteousness. If only it were so easy! Genuine initiates never make spectacular revelations, for not only do they know how difficult it is to reveal the truth, they also know how few human beings really want to hear it. And those who do want to hear rarely have the strength to bear it.

Truth is not a pill you can swallow or a magic formula that will instantly transform your understanding of reality. To be sure, an initiate continually reveals the truth, but the truths he reveals are the laws and methods that men and women need in order to work at their own transformation, for it is this preparatory work that will eventually give them access to the truth. What would happen if an initiate revealed the truth directly? In the first place, there are always some who are incapable of understanding whatever you tell them, and the initiate would only be wasting his time. Then there are those who distort what they hear and who, without realizing it, would use the knowledge for their own destruction and that of others. Finally, there are those who refuse the truth because it is inconvenient; it goes against what they judge to be their interests.

In other passages in the Gospels Jesus spoke of the difficulties encountered by those who try to reveal the truth. The parable of the sower is one example.

Behold a sower went forth to sow; And when he sowed, some seeds fell by the way side, and the fowls came and devoured them up: Some fell upon stony places, where they had not much earth: and forthwith they sprung up because they had no deepness of earth: And when the sun was up they were scorched; and because they had no root they withered away. And some fell among thorns; and the thorns sprung up, and choked them: But other fell into good ground, and brought forth fruit...

Hear ye therefore the parable of the sower. When any one heareth the word of the kingdom, and understandeth it not, then cometh the wicked one, and catcheth away that which was sown in his heart. This is he which received seed by the way side. But he that received the seed into stony places, the same is he that heareth the word, and anon with joy receiveth it; Yet he hath not root in himself, but dureth for a while: for when tribulation or persecution ariseth because of the word, by and by he is offended. He also that received seed among the thorns is he that heareth the word; and the care of this world, and the deceitfulness of riches, choke the word, and he becometh unfruitful. But he that received seed into the good ground is he that heareth the word and understandeth it.[1]

---

1 Matthew, 13, 3-8; 18-23.

On another occasion Jesus said: 'Give not that which is holy unto the dogs, neither cast ye your pearls before swine, lest they trample them under their feet, and turn again and rend you.'

The pearls that Jesus is speaking about are the truths that human beings are not ready for. If you try to reveal them, not only will people fail to appreciate them but they will turn against you. You must not imagine that it is enough for an initiate to come and reveal the truth for human beings to accept it. History shows us countless examples of those who dared to come with a message of truth and who were abused, tortured and crucified. Do you think that it would have made any difference if Jesus had answered Pilate's question about truth? Would Pilate have been persuaded not to hand him over to be sentenced to death? No, of course not. He was not ready to accept the truth.

Jesus gave his teaching and worked miracles in the presence of his disciples for no more than three years, so we need not be surprised if, at the end of this time, he said: 'I have yet many things to say unto you, but ye cannot bear them now.' This shows that during those three years with them he had done no more than prepare them to receive the Spirit of truth.

But let us pause for a moment and look at what Jesus said immediately after this: 'When he the Spirit of truth is come, he will guide you into all truth.'

This phrase contains a very important idea and I wonder if you have noticed it. It is this: in order to find truth we have to be guided, but guided, of course, by superior spirits who are capable of communicating their experience to us and of being our link with truth, with Christ, with God himself. All true guidance, knowledge and experience come from above. From the beginning of the world initiates and great masters have always handed on the same knowledge. They have always taught that life is a continuous chain, an uninterrupted hierarchy of beings reaching from the smallest atom all the way to the archangels and to God himself, and that each individual being is a constituent part of the immense living body of the universe. We all have our own appointed place in this great chain of beings; we are all linked to those above and those below. Whether we like it or not, this link exists, and it is essential to be aware of it and to work to reinforce our ties with those on a higher level who can lead us to ever greater heights.

Those who believe that their own personal experience is enough, that they can get along without being linked to the hierarchy of luminous spirits, will always be poor in true knowledge, while those who turn to the archives of the spirit for knowledge will become very rich. So Jesus was also saying this, that the truths that can save us have to be bequeathed to us by other, higher beings. If we had no friends in the higher world to hand on their spiritual treasures to us, we should be lost. But truth is revealed to us only to the extent that we love these beings of light. If we do not love them we shall never understand them, and truth will never come to dwell in us. Truth manifests itself in our lives in proportion to our love and wisdom.

'When the Comforter, the Spirit of truth is come...' Who or what is this Spirit of truth? There are, in fact, seven spirits before the throne of God.[2] They are the spirits of the seven lights or rays: the Spirit of life and love (the red ray); the Spirit of holiness (the orange ray); the Spirit of wisdom (the yellow ray); the Spirit of eternity (the green ray); the Spirit of truth (the blue ray); the Spirit of strength (the indigo ray), and the Spirit of divine love and of sacrifice (the violet ray). These are the seven spirits of the divine virtues. When the Spirit of truth descended into the spiritual bodies of Jesus' disciples, he worked wonders in them

---

2 See *The Spirits of the Seven Lights* in Complete Works, vol. 10.

and through them, driving out devils, healing the sick and raising the dead.

Christ's promise to his disciples was a promise to us also, and this means that if we want to be strong and enlightened we must ask God to send us his Spirit of truth. We could send him a message, something along these lines, for instance: 'Dear Lord, until now I have always wanted to be independent, because I thought that in this way I would become powerful and rich, but I now realize that it is just the opposite. I no longer want to be independent, for I find that I am weaker and poorer than before. Send me your Spirit of truth to guide me and teach me to distinguish truth from falsehood, so that I may avoid the dangers that surround me. Let my name be inscribed in your book as your servant.'

In the Cabbalah the Hebrew name for the Spirit of truth is *Ruah ha-Emeth*. You can communicate with this spirit by concentrating your mind on blue light. Imagine rays of blue light all round you, entering into you, and coursing through you. Little by little, you will have an extraordinary sense of peace, because peace is also associated with blue. When you are wrapped in this profound peace, passions die down, prejudices and biases drop away and you see reality more clearly; in this way you advance along the path of truth.

Gradually, if you persevere with these exercises, you will find that your faith in the power of the different colours grows and the results will be more substantial. This was my experience: through constant practice over many years, I discovered that a knowledge of the properties of the different rays and how to use them is a very exalted science. This science of light and colour was known to the hierophants of ancient times. It was also known to Christ, and one day everybody will be obliged to study it. The world was created by light, and by means of light man, too, can be a creator. Even if all the other sciences were to be lost, the science of light and colour would always remain, for the different colours represent the different virtues of light.

This is why you should also work with the yellow ray of wisdom and the red ray of love, so as to attract to yourself the blue ray of truth.

Chapter Eight

THREE LEVELS OF TRUTH

Many people think that just because an idea has occurred to them it is necessarily true. Unfortunately, there is no guarantee that this is so. Lunatics are also convinced of the truth of their ideas; in fact, no one is more convinced of the truth of his opinions than a lunatic!

If you sincerely want to know truth you must try to understand how cosmic intelligence envisages things, and you can do this by observing nature. This is how I test the truth of an idea: if nature approves of it I accept it as true; if she frowns on it I dismiss it as untrue. I never accept anything as true without looking to see what the great book of nature says about it. Does this astonish you? If so, I can only say that instead of remaining perpetually astonished you would do better to take this idea seriously and act on it. Always look for confirmation of your ideas in nature, in the mineral, vegetable, animal and human kingdoms, and even in the stars. If nature endorses your point of view the day will come sooner or later when the whole world will be obliged to accept it as true, for you will have all the power of nature behind you. But if nature does not agree with your theories she will not back them up and, even though the whole world acclaims them today, they will eventually collapse.

But truth, which is a philosophical problem, is also a practical problem. Why is this? Because when truth is confined to the mental plane it is incomplete. To be complete it needs to descend to the plane of feelings, and lower still, to the plane of action. One may be prepared to accept something as true theoretically, intellectually, because on the purely intellectual level everything is possible, everything is easy to accept. As long as it is only a theory it does not oblige us to commit ourselves. And this is why theoretical truth is insufficient; it has not reached the level of feelings or behaviour. In other words, it still has to be acted on and, of course, this is more complicated. Most people will readily admit, for instance, that all men are brothers, but they find it far more difficult to have brotherly feelings for all men. To behave as brothers is the most difficult thing in the world. Sadly, we have to recognize that it is the one thing we do least well.

So you see it is not enough to acknowledge that a truth exists as a principle on a higher level. For a truth to become true for us, we have to know it on the three levels: mental, emotional and physical. Only then can a truth be truly true. A truth sometimes appears to you in a sudden illumination. It shoots through you like a flash of lightning, overturning all your previous convictions and changing your whole outlook on life. Yes, but even though your whole being may have been turned upside down by a revelation it does not mean that this revelation has reached so deeply into the physical plane that you are instantly capable of manifesting that truth. You have been dazzled, you have pierced a mystery, but that still does not entitle you to say that you have grasped the truth. Too many indications in your everyday behaviour prove the contrary. It is only when you are capable of putting into practice what you have understood that you can really say that you understand: that you understand three times over, on three levels; that you understand in the three worlds. It is very important to have a clear idea of these three levels of comprehension: the intellectual, the emotional and the physical.

I have so often heard people saying, 'I understand, I understand,' and then I see them doing the exact opposite of what they thought they had understood. You can never claim to have understood an idea as long as you are content to accept it on the intellectual level and make no attempt to put it into practice. One of the essential points of our teaching is the necessity of giving priority to the tangible realization of truth.

Truth must be eaten, drunk and breathed; only in this way can it become visible and tangible through your actions. A truth that is not acted upon is almost useless. What is the good of having sublime convictions if you behave like an animal?

If you are really sincere in your desire to nourish true thoughts, you will feel the need to make your actions match your thoughts. If you do not feel this need it means that you are not really convinced. It is no use trying to fool yourself; as long as you do not act in accordance with what you know, it means that something is missing in your knowledge. It is very bad to encourage human beings in the false belief that there is nothing to worry about if their actions fail to conform to their thoughts. A genuine initiatic teaching is concerned with every aspect of human nature and all the different activities corresponding to each aspect. The quest for truth, which is the whole purpose of initiation, concerns man in his entirety; not only in his psychic life but also in all his down-to-earth physical activities, such as eating, sleeping, washing, walking, and so on.

It is not only a few brain cells that are called on to comprehend truth. The intellect is not enough; our whole body has to co-operate. Every tiny cell, not only in the brain but also in the heart and lungs, and even the feet, must contribute to the knowledge of truth, so that the soul and spirit may absorb all these elements and communicate them to the brain. Truth can only be grasped by the whole being. Our whole being has to be stirred, to vibrate and resuscitate.

I have sometimes been criticized for neglecting many aspects of philosophy or initiatic science. Well, in the first place, let me say that I deliberately neglect them in my own life, so it is not surprising that I should not try to interest you in them. In my youth — and later, too — I read a great many books. I thought that nothing was more important than to study, to learn, to know everything. I was passionately interested in all the most abstract problems of initiatic science. Then, gradually, thanks to the influence of my master, Peter Deunov, I understood that this was not what really mattered. The only thing that really

matters in life is to live. And to live is to
manifest oneself on the physical plane, to relate
to and communicate with people and things.
We do not need all kinds of abstract theories to
do this; we only need to know and apply a few
simple truths.

Your knowledge must be lived in order to
remain within you for all eternity. The only
thing that will not disappear, the only thing you
can take with you into the next world, is
knowledge that you have proved for yourself
and put into practice in your own life;
knowledge that has become part of your very
flesh. This is why initiates endeavour to
concentrate on the essential and to incarnate it
in their lives. They leave aside all that is
inessential, knowing that even if they did not
do so deliberately today they would be obliged
to do so one day when they left this world. And
you, too, must understand why you should live
your knowledge, why it must be something that
you touch and taste and put into practice until
you sense that it becomes part of your own
quintessence. If you succeed in this, not only
will no one ever be able to take your
knowledge away from you in this life, but you
will still have it when you come back to earth
in your next incarnation.

Now, I am not saying that you should not
read or study. On the contrary, it is very

necessary to do so. Even in an initiatic teaching you have to begin by becoming acquainted with ideas. As you are not yet capable of truly feeling and living the truths that are revealed to you, you must begin by knowing and understanding them intellectually. The great difference between a spiritual master and other teachers is that a spiritual master will always urge you to put the greatest emphasis on life. He will give you some materials, but you are not meant to tuck them away in your head and keep them there; you must begin to build something with them. Otherwise you will have to start from the beginning and study the same things over and over again in each incarnation and will never get any further. As a matter of fact, this is the great weakness of all highly educated people: they make use of their knowledge to talk, write and teach, but never to build and consolidate themselves, so that, in spite of all their erudition, one senses a certain fragility and lack of consistency in them.

Do you understand now why I am always urging you not to be content to record ideas? Why I am always telling you that you must feel and taste them? And you must not only taste them, you must also put them into practice and realize them.

Chapter Nine

BE FAITHFUL TO THE TRUTH

First of all we have to understand where truth lies, and once we have understood this we must be faithful to it and work at it with tenacity, perseverance and patience. Otherwise what good can it do us? It is not enough to find the truth if we then do nothing with it — or do nothing more than preach about what we think we have found. In any case, to find the truth is a work that is never ended, for we can never hope to know all there is to know about it.

Many people decide to learn a musical instrument because they have been moved by a piece of music heard at a concert. They practise for a few days and then forget about it for a week or more. Again, they practise for a few days and again they abandon it. And so it goes on for a little while until their lack of perseverance leads them to give it up altogether. And many people are thrilled by the truth just as others are thrilled by music; but their enthusiasm does not last and they cease to pursue it as soon as they feel that it is becoming too difficult for them. Unfortunately, we have to admit that perseverance and fidelity are not the most common of human qualities. But in a disciple, a candidate for initiation, it is precisely these qualities that are required.

In ancient Egypt an initiate was considered to have achieved his greatest victory when he could say of himself: 'I am stable, son of one who is stable, conceived and engendered in the realm of stability.' Egyptian pharaohs and divinities were often portrayed seated on a cubic block of stone which represented stability, for with its six identical square surfaces a cube provides a more stable physical foundation than any other solid form. This posture is characteristic of the spirit of Egyptian culture, and it is very different from what we see in India, where divinities and sages are usually portrayed sitting cross-legged on the ground in the lotus position. The lotus position expresses receptivity and a mystical sensibility. With the Egyptians, by contrast, the emphasis was on will-power and activity. The cube gave them stability and at the same time incited them to action, for one is more dynamic when seated on a cubic block of stone than cross-legged on the ground.

But we must not spend too much time on this question of symbols, for the subject is so vast and complex that it is not possible to get to the bottom of it. Rather, let us concentrate on the quality of stability, for stability is the very essence of God. God is by essence immutable, unchanging. He is absolute and eternal love; absolute and eternal wisdom. Although his manifestations and forms are infinite in number and variety, his essence is unique and changeless.

It is essential for a disciple who has found the path of truth and righteousness to strive for stability, but this does not mean that he has to be rigid, obstinate and inflexible. On the contrary, to be stable means to manifest oneself with open-mindedness and flexibility while remaining faithful to one's ideal and inner orientation. To be stable means to be true to one's convictions, to one's inner loyalties. The luminous entities of the invisible world lose confidence in those who neglect or betray their ideal. They are always ready to help and encourage us, but only if we are unswervingly loyal to our convictions. Those who are unstable cannot be entrusted with the key to the mysteries — the key which resembles the symbol of Venus and which one sees in the hands of the Egyptian initiates.

I know that you do not particularly enjoy hearing about fidelity and stability. It seems so dull and you feel the need for variety. But what makes you so sure that stability and fidelity are incompatible with variety? You are free to change anything you please as long as you do not change your basic orientation. Personally, I like change and variety as much as anyone; I am all for it, but not any and every change. I am for outer diversity and inner unity.

As I say, we have to understand where truth lies and, once we understand this, never deviate from it. Even if you are not immediately capable of bringing your behaviour into line with the truth you have found, that is no reason to deny or forsake it. If you are sincere in your search you must never allow the difficulties you meet, however great, to cause you to abandon the truth in favour of something easier and more agreeable. There may be times when you are obliged to relax your efforts, but that does not mean that you have to lose sight of your ultimate goal. You must not use a moment of fatigue or weakness as a pretext for changing your basic orientation. Nobody will blame you if you are tired; when you are tired you must rest but without abandoning your chosen path. You do not need a change of direction in order to rest. The most dangerous thing in life is to abandon your philosophy on the pretext that you are not always capable of living up to it.

Let us look at the case of a man who has been working for an ideal for years and has proved himself to be unselfish and generous and willing to make whatever sacrifices are called for. Well, we all know what happens in cases like this: there are always some who are ungrateful or who exploit his generosity, and there may come a time when he is tempted to throw the whole thing overboard. He tells himself, 'Why am I always fair game for everybody? I should have realized long ago that life was a jungle and that I could not get anywhere unless I cheated and schemed unscrupulously like everyone else. What an idiot I am! I have had enough: from now on I'm going to be like them.' No decision could be based on a more foolish argument. It is extremely painful to lose your illusions — no one knows this better than I — but why add to this loss by depriving yourself of your ideal as well? Why cast aside the one thing that can give meaning to your life? Henceforth, when other people disappoint you, shed a few tears if you must, but never think that you were wrong to choose the divine path of kindness, generosity and sacrifice, for this is the path of truth and you must never forsake it.

It is true that life often places us in circumstances that unsettle and confuse us, and we do not know what we should do. But the fact that you do not know what to do is no justification for casting aside what you know to be true. On the contrary, it is at moments like this that you must cleave to what you know with even greater fidelity. It is no good deluding yourselves: the circumstances of life will never conform completely to your desires or needs. It is up to you to find the attitude that will enable you to find solutions to all your difficulties and remedies for all your ills. It is no use moaning, 'Oh, why are people like that? Why does this have to happen to me? Why is life so difficult?' Those are not the questions you should be asking yourself. The questions you should be asking yourself are these: 'What am I meant to understand from what has happened? How can I transform this circumstance and use it to advance my own evolution and help others?' It is questions like these that will help you to make progress and become stronger whatever your circumstances. Always remind yourself that the invisible world does not put you in a difficult situation in order to throw you off balance, but in order to help you to understand certain realities and develop certain virtues. If you follow this line of reasoning you will grow constantly in self-reliance and stability.

I repeat: once you have understood where the truth lies, nothing must be allowed to make you change your mind or abandon your chosen path. Heaven will not judge you too severely if you are unable to behave every day with the same uncompromising harmony, purity and integrity. But if you abandon your 'first love', if you stop believing in harmony, purity and justice, heaven will not forgive you. Heaven loves those who are capable of fidelity in the face of adversity, those who continue to learn, to understand, and to use and overcome difficulties in order to keep advancing.

There, this is what matters: to be faithful to the truth and to keep advancing.

Chapter Ten

THERE IS NO ARGUING ABOUT TASTES

Suppose you live in a beautiful mansion and you invite some friends to stay for a few days. For their benefit you organize walks in the park, concerts, delicious meals, and other forms of entertainment, and you know in advance that, depending on their individual temperaments and tastes, each of your guests will prefer a different aspect of what you offer them. But you are confident that they will all appreciate the comfort, the variety and freshness of the food, the music, light and colour, the fresh air and the pleasant company. And then what happens? To your distress, you start hearing all kinds of criticisms and complaints: some say that they are not used to the food; one has indigestion, another complains of a bilious attack. Some catch a cold from too much fresh air; others complain that the light is too bright; for others the company is fatiguing, and some even get a headache when they listen to the music. What can you do or say to save the situation? You wanted to give them all pleasure and you have failed miserably. What is wrong with all these people? They are ill, that is what is wrong with them. And since they are ill you cannot rely on their judgement.

Of course, this is simply an example of how people behave. Perhaps it is a little exaggerated — but only a little — for it is true to say that in their inner life most human beings react like those sick people: wisdom bores them; patience irritates them; kindness seems stupid; fairness is too much of an effort; purity is insipid. As for love, they are interested in it only if it means that others love them and are willing to make every sacrifice for their sake.

Nobody would admit it, of course, but it is true to say that people's opinions depend more often than not on their physical or psychic weaknesses; on their passions and baser appetites. And, unfortunately, this applies with equal truth to artists, thinkers and writers. Their point of view is largely determined by their personal weaknesses and vices. They are certainly sincere when they tell you that their philosophy or their conception of art is the fruit of long years of reflection, but the truth is that all these theories are simply the expression of their moods and of their unhealthy and sometimes vicious inclinations. It is particularly striking to see how those who are most strongly persuaded of the objectivity and disinterestedness of their opinions about life's problems are precisely those on whom their instinctive tendencies have the strongest hold.

This attitude is already discernible in children. When a woman forbids her little boy to glut himself on sweets, jam, or cakes, he says that she is naughty; and he is persuaded that it is true. And although his desires and needs change as the years go by and he reaches old age, they continue to reflect his instinctive tendencies and tastes. Yes, as I have said, almost all ideologies and philosophical systems stem from the needs of human beings, and very often from their lowest and least glorious needs.

Take the question of sexuality. As the majority of men and women are incapable of controlling their sexual impulses, self-styled specialists have elaborated convenient theories and laid down rules about sexual behaviour. But these rules and theories have absolutely no objective value; they only apply to those weak, ignorant men and women who do not know — and do not want to know — that sexual energy can be a very powerful ally in the spiritual life, and that they should be using it to evolve spiritually instead of squandering it in the pursuit of pleasure. And the same kind of thing goes on in all the other areas of life. This is why it is so difficult to instruct human beings and get them to accept initiatic truths.

Perhaps you will object that there are people whose reaction to initiatic truth is the opposite. Yes, that is true. It does not happen very often, unfortunately, but there are people who, when they are exposed to the truths of the spiritual world for the first time, have the overwhelming impression that they are on home ground, that they already know these things. Although they have never had any conscious experience of them before, they sense that they are familiar. This is a very interesting psychic phenomenon, and I think it is worth taking a few moments to talk about it.

Before beginning the long journey away from their heavenly homeland, human beings dwelt in the bosom of the eternal Lord, and the memory of that first paradise lives on to this day as a faint and distant glimmer of light in their minds. In reality, this light is not distant; it is within each one of us. It only seems distant because it exists on the causal plane. As human beings gradually moved down through the mental, astral, etheric and physical planes and became more deeply immersed in matter, they had many experiences which were entirely new to them and which gradually obscured the memory of that light. However, human beings do not all experience exactly the same things in the course of their reincarnations. Some lose their way and wander on dark and devious paths, while others manage to keep deep within themselves a certain awareness of their divine origin. This is why they immediately recognize an initiatic truth when it is revealed to them; it awakens the echo of something familiar and they sense that it cannot be anything but true. But those who have lost their way and allowed themselves to be led into a state of disorder and chaos are impervious to such revelations. They will only be able to open their minds to them if they make the effort to take the upward path again by seeking to purify themselves and entertain nobler thoughts and feelings.

We have all been made in the same way; we are all designed to understand and live the same divine realities. On the surface, however, it is the differences and contradictions that are most clearly visible, leading to all kinds of misunderstandings and conflicts. Of course, we all agree that we have certain fundamental needs in common (to eat, drink, sleep, bring children into the world, and so on), but in every other area it is the confusion of the Tower of Babel, and most people find this normal. They say sententiously, 'There is no arguing about tastes', (and to show off their erudition they say it in Latin: *De gustibus non disputandum*). This is the equivalent of saying that everyone has his own form of madness and has the right to do whatever that madness dictates!

The truth is that human beings are torn between two contradictory tendencies: on the one hand they tend to imitate others, and on the other they want to show that they are different. Very often this leads them to imitate others in their least desirable habits, and to differ from them in areas where they should be in harmony with them. It is precisely in this spirit of contradiction that human beings are most alike. If you really want to be different from others you should imitate the tiny minority of sages whose sole preoccupation is to establish peace and harmony within themselves and in the world around them. This is the way of a disciple, and in this way he becomes very different from most people, while at the same time he comes to understand them and to understand all their suffering and sickness and anxieties. Those who resemble each other have no real understanding of each other: they all suffer from the same ills, but as they are all wrapped up in their personal problems they are incapable of putting themselves in someone else's place. Why? Because they have chosen the wrong people to imitate, those who are inconsiderate and selfish.

Everybody says, 'To my mind it is thus and so... My opinion is this or that...' Yes, that is all very well, but they should have some consideration for the opinions of others also. Each one is in the right from his own point of view, but the right of each one makes for an overall wrong, an overall state of conflict. 'Such is the way of the world,' they say as it goes from one conflict to another. The extraordinary thing is that at the same time everybody regrets the absence of peace and deplores the fact that it seems impossible to settle things peacefully. They even find cause for astonishment in this and, naturally, they blame everyone but themselves. They fail to understand that the situation is what it is because individuals refuse to examine the origin of their opinions, or to question the premises on which they are based. And yet it should be obvious to them that there are many occasions in life when very small details can cloud their vision and warp their judgement: a cold in the head impairs their sense of taste or smell; toothache makes them incapable of thought, and alcohol distorts their vision to such an extent that if they drive after drinking they are liable to kill themselves and others.

There are thousands of physical — and especially psychic — circumstances in everyday life which prevent us from evaluating events and situations correctly. We think that we are being objective and impartial when in reality we are largely dependent on external conditions: heredity, education, social standing, the people we associate with and our physical and psychic health. If you have had a sleepless night or missed a meal, everything seems to irritate you; if you are promoted at work, everything in the garden is lovely; if you quarrel with your husband or wife, everyone suddenly seems detestable. Having seen how vicious and immoral someone is you have a very poor opinion of him, and then one day he sends you a magnificent present — are you sure that your opinion of him will not change? It is normal for our judgements and opinions to be influenced by circumstances, but we must be conscious of this influence and not give in to it blindly. For what is the value of a truth that depends on external conditions and personal points of view?

We must have our own personal truth, to be sure, but we must never lose sight of the fact that truth depends neither on conditions nor on persons. It is a common failing of human beings to attach importance to what someone says only in proportion to his rank or social standing. You pay no attention to a truth if it is revealed to you by a pauper, but you are all ears if that same truth — or, for that matter, any trivial piece of information — is revealed to you by a distinguished professor. And yet truth has its own intrinsic value, and it is this that we should appreciate, regardless of the form in which it is revealed, or the title or rank of the person who reveals it.

The value of a truth is not lessened by being spoken by someone of no importance, any more than the value of a gold sovereign is diminished by being in the pocket of a tramp. Naturally, if a king gives you a sovereign it will represent something more than its face-value for you, because your vanity is involved. It contains not a milligram of gold more than any other similar coin, but you can say, 'It was a present from the king!' You may even get a better price for it, just as furniture or other antiques fetch a better price if they belonged to Napoleon, Balzac or Madame de Staël. But that is nothing but snobbery! A scientific or philosophical truth has an intrinsic value even if it is not spoken by an initiate. If you are sufficiently highly evolved not to dwell on the form, you will pay as much attention to a truth that is spoken by a peasant as to one that is spoken by a king.

So from time to time pause and ask yourself what it is that makes you accept or reject an idea or opinion. Try to recognize the inner tendencies which prevent you from judging impartially, and stop behaving as though you were in possession of the whole truth. It is essential that human beings make up their minds to reason along these lines and be a little less self-assertive, for until they do they will continue to quarrel about anything and everything. You must learn to recognize all those inferior tendencies that reinforce your false opinions, for it is they that make it impossible to recapture the unity in which human beings can understand each other and coexist harmoniously.

Above all, stop hiding behind the notion that there is no arguing about tastes. Of course, this does not mean that those who possess the truths of initiatic science have a right to be intolerant of other people's opinions and to impose certain ideas or rules on them. No, you must not interfere with other people. It is within yourself that you have to be convinced that a norm does exist by which opinions and tastes can be judged. That which is good and beautiful should be good and beautiful for everyone. Each individual is free to have his own tastes as far as quantities are concerned, but not in what concerns the quality. We should all always choose what is pure, luminous and divine.

There are multitudes of angels and archangels in the universe, and nobody is going to reproach you for choosing one particular angel rather than another; also, you are free to spend as much time as you please with the angel of your choice. But heaven will reproach you if, for the sake of change or because you think it would be more original or exciting, you decide to make friends with a devil.

Chapter Eleven

REALITY: OBJECTIVE AND SUBJECTIVE

Generally speaking, people tend to believe that material objects are perceived in exactly the same way by everybody. Nobody is likely to look at a water melon, for instance, and say that it is a cat or a piano, but there may be some disagreement about its colour (even for those who are not colour-blind), and depending on the size and strength of the individual looking at it, its size and weight will be evaluated differently. If you want the objective truth, you are going to need some instruments: a weighing machine or a tape measure, for instance. A human being can never be totally objective.

When someone describes an event he has witnessed you want him to state the facts exactly as they happened, without letting his personal impressions get in the way. In one way you are right to demand this, because if he begins describing his feelings, reactions, and impressions you will not learn exactly what happened. On the other hand, in asking him to confine his description to a factual account of the words, acts, times and distances involved, as though it had all been recorded by a camera, you will learn about only one aspect of the reality and the story will still be incomplete.

Truth does not exist only in the form, in the physical elements which can be observed. It is also within us and in all that surrounds us, in that intangible flow of inner life which radiates and emanates from all people and things. If you can neither see nor feel this life how can you describe or explain it? And how can you truly claim to be objective?

But what does it mean to be 'objective'? And why are people so distrustful of subjectivity? When we pit objectivity against subjectivity we are pitting the outer world against the inner world as though they were mutually exclusive. Perhaps an example will make this clearer. Imagine a large spherical construction with one person on the inside and another on the outside. If you ask each one in turn to describe the shape of the sphere, the one on the outside will say that the walls are convex, whereas the one on the inside will say that they are concave. And how should we interpret this? The person on the outside is the intellect, which studies objective reality; the person on the inside is the heart, which gives priority to subjective reality. Which of them is right? Both of them possess fifty per cent of the truth, but as neither is willing to make the effort to understand the other's point of view, they will argue and quarrel about it endlessly until a third principle intervenes and gets them to understand that neither can see more than half the truth. If you want to know the whole truth of something, you have to be on the inside as well as on the outside.

You will ask, 'But who or what is capable of seeing things from the inside and the outside simultaneously? It is impossible.' No, it is very difficult, certainly, but not impossible. Intuition has this power, for intuition is at the same time understanding and sensation, and for this reason it is capable of seeing the whole reality at a glance. Intuition is capable of uniting intellect and heart, thought and feeling, wisdom and love in the quest for truth.

The conflict between heart and intellect can be seen in the enmity that has pitted religion against science for so many centuries. The realm of science is the outer, objective world, whereas that of religion is the inner, subjective world. And when I say 'religion' I am not talking about the dozens of rational or irrational doctrines and rites which people have been forced to accept on pain of fearful retribution.

No, religion in the broad sense is the authentic mystical sensation which convinces those who experience it that the inner life is the only true life.

We have to realize, of course, that the exploration of the inner world is difficult and fraught with danger. And it is precisely because of the danger that initiatic science is so necessary, for it teaches a disciple that he cannot reach the bright heavenly regions of intuition without first traversing the shadowy regions of the astral and lower mental planes, in which all is illusion and error. I have often talked to you about these murky regions, saying that they are like zones of fog or dust.[1] Fog represents the raw emotions of the heart, and dust represents the errors of the intellect. And the danger is that one can get lost and linger indefinitely in these regions, for the fog and dust make it impossible to see one's way clearly. Only those who manage to make their way out of these regions succeed in reaching the peak of the spiritual mountain, the causal plane.

An initiatic teaching does not only tell you about the different worlds that exist; it also gives you the criteria you need to evaluate your own states of mind, your own thoughts and

---

1 See Chap. 3 of *Looking into the Invisible*, Izvor Collection, No. 228.

emotions. It gives you the methods you need to develop the spiritual organs that will enable you to make your way through these regions of illusory perceptions and reach the regions of the soul and spirit. If you work and practise perseveringly, the day will come when you will see the things of the psychic world with the same clarity, the same accuracy and precision, as you see those of the physical world. When this day comes you will see life as it really is; you will see things in their entirety. If you have to explain or describe something, you will be able to give an accurate picture of reality, because you will not be speaking of your own personal perception; your explanations will not be confined to the outer appearance of things.

When I speak of the importance of the subjective world, therefore, I am not saying that we have to disregard objective reality and allow ourselves to be swayed by every notion that enters our minds. Quite the opposite, in fact! I know as well as you do that in the minds of most people subjectivity is synonymous with personal opinion based on prejudice and illusion, and that this kind of subjectivity can lead to very grave aberrations. For those who have never made the slightest effort to master their own thoughts and feelings the subjective world is a dense and inextricable forest in which they lose their way. But for those who have worked perseveringly and have succeeded in rising above this region in their own inner lives, the subjective world is, on the contrary, the world of light and certainty.

You can now see how important it is to be very vigilant and get into the habit of scrutinizing all your thoughts and feelings so as not to lose your way. Most human beings know nothing of the psychic world and its structures. Thoughts, feelings, sensations and desires flow in and out of them, and they accept everything that comes without asking too many questions. They have little idea that these psychic phenomena correspond to certain regions of which they are, as it were, both the inhabitants and the messengers. Even less does it ever occur to them that they themselves have some work to do in these areas. The result is that some fall victim to their illusions, while others, in an effort to avoid the same fate, cling to what they call 'the objective world'. Unfortunately for them, this is not the way to reach a clear vision of reality! There can be no clarity of vision in the objective world except to the extent that man is capable of projecting light from himself into this world. Without this illumination, this beacon, this ray of light from his subjective world, man can have no true perception of the objective world. Light is not inherent in the objective world; unless we cast our own ray of light into it, we shall never be capable of understanding it.

Think about this for a moment and you will see that this is true: without the psychic life, without the subjective life of thoughts and feelings, what objective reality is there? None; even the objective world disappears. It is thanks to your subjective life that the objective life, which you value so highly, continues to exist. Get rid of your subjective life and you would be dead — and for the dead there is neither subjectivity nor objectivity. It is all over. It is for the living that there is something that we call the objective world: the sun, the stars, trees and mountains. And this means that if you focus all your attention on the objective world in the hope of finding a refuge in it, you will actually be alienating yourself from light and life and will never find truth.

It is impossible to be completely objective, because the objective world is always something external, something alien to yourself. If you ask someone to be absolutely objective, it is as though you asked him to stop being himself! It is just not possible. You cannot not be yourself, therefore you cannot not be subjective. Do not ask others to be objective; ask them rather to give up their lower subjectivity and rise to a higher subjectivity.

If you want to cling to the objective world, you are, of course, perfectly free to do so. You will find a form of truth there, too, but only a very limited form, for above and beyond what we see and hear there are so many other things going on, things that can only be perceived if we develop eyes and ears and a brain of another, higher kind.

There are two kinds of truth: a rich, living truth for those who are capable of sensing the reality that lies beyond physical appearances; and a threadbare truth for those who sense nothing, who have shut and locked their doors and windows, and locked their truth in with them. The only truth is the truth that belongs to us! To this you will object that when we talk of truth we are talking about a reality that has its own independent existence. Yes, I agree. But we can only perceive and know that objective reality if we process it, as it were, through our own subjectivity. It is we who mould and fashion it by adding or taking from it elements of our own. There are only subjective truths.

How do you explain, for example, the fact that scientists have never been able to agree about the existence of God? Is this not rather extraordinary? Here you have a group of people with the same scientific training, the same brain-power, and the same material elements on which to base their theories, and yet they all reach different conclusions. In the harmony, the extraordinary variety and marvellous organization of matter, some sense the presence of a Creator whom they revere and adore; others see nothing more than a finely adjusted mechanism which they attribute to chance. Surely this is proof enough that material, objective reality can only be seen through the lens of individual subjectivity.

Perhaps you will say that scientists who are materialists are at least honest, for they only deal with what they can actually see and touch. Well, call this honesty if you like, but, for my part, I would say it was a limitation, a sign of narrow-mindedness, for it boils down to saying that they only deal with outward appearances. And yet scientists are more aware than others of how deceptive appearances can be. The best known example of this deception is that of the sun and stars, which seem to revolve round the earth. There are a great many people, even today, who believe that this is true; that the sun really does revolve round the earth. And for centuries any scientist who denied this was risking his life. Remember Galileo!

If we want to see the truth, we must not cling to what is before our eyes but move about and look at things from different points of view; abandon the point of view of matter and see things from the point of view of the spirit.

Materialistic philosophy is based on a knowledge of matter as perceived by the five senses, and it is therefore false, because it is based on appearances alone. Appearances have their use, of course, but we must not be deceived by them. They are there to make us think about things, as clues to help us to find our way to truth. We have to work with appearances, but we must never allow ourselves to be paralysed by them, for it is this that leads to spiritual death.

What do initiates say about this? They teach that the higher a human being rises in the subjective world — that is to say, in the spiritual world — the more clearly he sees and the more capable he becomes of discerning the true nature of what he sees. He becomes so pure and transparent that reality passes through his psychic world without being distorted. His inner subjectivity and the objective reality of the universe coincide. He becomes capable of knowing truth. We can know truth only when we rid ourselves of all the inner elements that warp and distort reality. It is our inner, spiritual progress, therefore, that makes it possible for us gradually to discover truth, for all knowledge necessarily passes through our subjectivity; it is our subjectivity that illuminates or obscures reality. Only those who have attained perfection can know absolute truth. Until we reach perfection we can only flounder in error and approximations.

Chapter Twelve

THE PRIMACY OF SUBJECTIVE REALITY

Our physical body is capable of growth and development because our inner life penetrates and vivifies it ever more fully. There comes a time, of course, when the body stops growing, but it continues to change and develop until the end of its days because the life-principle continues to penetrate it. Man forms his own body and he is tied to it by a network of subtle relationships which enable him to influence it. And this fact demonstrates a law which we must never lose sight of: we can only influence something to the extent to which we penetrate it. The reason why man cannot influence the objects around him to the same degree is that he has not built this kind of relationship with them; he does not penetrate them as he penetrates his body.

The close link between the life within us and our physical body is particularly evident in what we call psychosomatic reactions. A remark made in public or an emotion felt in private can make a person's face blush or turn white, yellow or green. And think of the effect that sometimes follows the unexpected news of a tragic or a joyful event: even without witnessing the event itself, the emotion can be so great to those who receive the news that they may faint or have a heart attack. And yet, what is a piece of news? How can something non-material affect someone to the point of depriving them of health, sanity or even life — or, on the contrary, of producing a miraculous cure?

Picture a mother who has been paralysed for years: one night a fire breaks out in the house and her child is asleep in another room. The thought that her child could be burnt alive is such a shock that she is capable of running into the bedroom to pick it up and carry it to safety. Under the influence of her love, the contact between her nervous system and her muscles is suddenly restored. Such a thing happens very rarely, to be sure, but it has happened. Why does nobody ever think of studying phenomena of this kind? You will perhaps say that they are already well known. Perhaps, but no one has ever studied them sufficiently in depth to learn how to use them in order to remedy certain physical or psychic problems.

But let me get back to the idea that we can only influence what we penetrate, for in this lies the mystery of creation. We say that God created the world out of nothing. In reality, God created the universe by drawing something from himself, by emanating or projecting outward some element of his own quintessence, and it is this quintessence that gradually condensed and formed what we now call matter. This process of creation brings us back to the question of the subjective and the objective worlds. Sometimes certain words or expressions are used so often that we lose sight of their original meaning; this is true in the case of the words subjective and objective. Subjective refers to a subject, and objective refers to an object. In the context of creation, God is the subject; in fact, we can say that he is the only subject in creation, whereas creation itself represents the objective world. But God created man in his own image, so man, too, is a subject who works on matter to mould and fashion it. To be sure, man does not create matter, but he creates the material conditions in which he lives in the world.

I know how difficult it will be for you to recognize the truth of this, for most of you believe that it is your material conditions that determine the rest. You think that the objective determines the subjective, that is to say, that your psychic states are the result of material elements and conditions. It is true that this often appears to be the case; many indications seem to point to this, but only because you look at the consequences rather than the causes; you look only at the final stages of a long process. If you want to see reality as it is, you must turn round and go back to the source, for everything comes from the one source.

Man came to earth by clothing himself in successive layers of increasingly dense matter, which initiatic science calls bodies. These bodies, starting with the subtlest and working down to the most densely material, are known as atmic, buddhic, causal, mental, astral and physical. The physical body, therefore, is the last of the mantles in which man clothed himself. And as his spirit descended ever deeper into matter, it became increasingly subject to limitations, but these limitations were of its own choosing. If, while descending to the level of matter, man had managed to maintain his links with the higher regions, he would not now be so crippled and hemmed in. Human beings complain that it is their material conditions that dictate their situation, but this is so only because their subjective dimension has abdicated, and now, having made their bed, as the saying goes, it only remains for them to lie on it.

When you cannot see the true origin of something you cannot avoid drawing false conclusions. But now that you know about these things, if you truly wish to transform yourselves, you will begin to see that your subjective dimension — your spirit and soul, your thoughts and your will — is capable of fashioning the objective dimension; is capable, that is, of transfiguring the conditions in which you live. Little by little, you will regain the powers that you possessed at the beginning, before sinking to the level of matter. This is the object of our hope. This is our salvation. Why is it so difficult to understand this?

It is entirely to your advantage to accept this philosophy. Even if it were not one hundred per cent true, it would be worth far more than all those stupid theories of materialistic science based only on outward appearances. Voltaire said that if God did not exist we should have to invent him! And what I say is that even if this philosophy of the primacy of the spirit were false, there would still be a million good reasons for adopting it. It is this philosophy that will enable you to grow out of your weaknesses and overcome difficulties. I could give you many examples of this, but one will be enough.

Picture a man who is living in great inconvenience and discomfort in a miserable hut of mud and straw that he has built for himself. What is the cause of his unhappiness? The objective reality of his wretched hut, or his own subjective reality; that is to say, he himself who created this situation? It is he who is responsible, of course. For whatever reason — incompetence, weakness or sloth — it is he who has put himself in these wretched circumstances. Perhaps you will feel inclined to say that if he was incapable of doing better it must be because his family was very poor and he had no education. In other words, you say, it is the objective aspect that determines his situation. Ah, but you are still looking only at the outward appearances! The fact that he incarnated in that particular family means that he had never done anything in his previous incarnation to deserve better. And so, you see, we are obliged to recognize that it is the subjective aspect that controls and guides events. You can say the same about those who marry and who, shortly afterwards, are heard to complain that their domestic life is intolerable. At first sight it might seem that it is the objective aspect that makes them suffer — their husband or wife, their mother-in-law, and so on — but this is not the case; it is the subjective aspect that is responsible for their situation, for each individual creates his own predicament.

Have you ever seen a bag of cement? It comes in the form of a dust which is so fine that it can be blown away by the slightest breeze. Mix it with water, however (and what is more fluid than water?), and it becomes a plastic paste. But beware of stepping in that paste, for if you do, before you know it, your foot will be held fast in it, and someone will have to come and break it up in order to release you — and you may well be injured in the process. Well, this is what happens with our destiny. The conditions of our present life are simply the concrete materialization of our psychic life, of our thoughts and feelings. Whose fault is it if we now find that our feet are caught in a block of cement? Man creates his own destiny, and having created it, he has to live in it and be subject to it, dependent on it. But the fact that his foot is inescapably caught in the cement is no reason to conclude that it is the cement that created his foot.

The whole of life points to this truth, but human beings have still not seen or understood it; they continue to confuse cause and consequence. To be sure, a consequence may become the cause of a succession of other consequences, but we must never lose sight of the fact that the original cause of things is never material; it is in the mind of man. This is why, instead of perpetually blaming your family, or social and political conditions, you should tell yourself, 'You poor dunce, if you were a little more intelligent, you would not be in such a pickle. You had better start looking for the cause of your joys and sorrows, your successes and failures, inside yourself instead of on the outside.'

The cause of your present difficulties may not have been formed by you in this incarnation; it may date back to a previous incarnation, but this makes no difference. The important thing is to understand that it is always you yourself who are the determining factor. As long as you refuse to acknowledge that it is you who are responsible, you will continue to work against your own best interests and will never be in control. On the other hand, once you realize that it all depends on you, you will have the reins of your destiny in your hands.

Chapter Thirteen

SCIENTIFIC PROGRESS
v.
MORAL PROGRESS

It is easy to see why the physical world holds such fascination for man: nature possesses such an abundance of riches. From the stones of earth to the stars in the heavens, the number and variety of things to see and study and analyse is infinite, and the sophisticated instruments that exist today make it even more alluring. Thousands and millions of scientists could spend all their days and nights studying the universe... there is enough to keep them happily occupied until the end of the world! But when the Creator gave man the five senses he needed in order to explore the physical world, he also gave him other instruments for the exploration of his inner world. The fact that man possesses these two kinds of instruments indicates that they are both necessary in order to see the whole of reality. It only remains for him to maintain them in working order within himself.

Certainly, the physical world is easier to study than the inner world. It is possible to determine the exact shape and size and weight of each element, and it is not difficult to get people to agree about numbers and forms. But how can you draw a map of the world of the soul and spirit? How can you weigh or measure or draw a line round a state of mind, a thought or a feeling? And yet this is precisely where the inner world has the advantage over the outer world: as nothing about it is material, it is invulnerable to attack from the outside. No one can seize your thoughts or feelings or beliefs. Your books, your laboratories and all your other material possessions can be taken away from you, but even if you are put in prison, no one can prevent you from feeling rich and free inside yourself; no one can prevent you from continuing to reflect and carry out experiments in your own inner laboratories.

I am sure you would all say that scientific progress was important. Yes, of course. Scientific progress has brought us comfort and security; it has made travel and communications easier; it has given us more medicines and more sophisticated machines in the home, as well as in schools, factories and hospitals. True, but when you think about it you realize that all these signs of progress concern only the material world, and for this very reason they have a debilitating and soporific effect on those who have no spiritual activity to counterbalance them.

I remember that a few years after World War II a group of Tibetan lamas visited Paris. As they were from a country which was considered to be very backward from the technological point of view, their hosts thought to impress them by taking them to see all the latest marvels of Western technology. To the astonishment of their guides, however, the Tibetans expressed neither surprise nor praise, and when asked for their comments they said that they saw no reason to be lost in admiration of these machines, for far from freeing man, they would most certainly make him their slave. This is a problem that troubles more and more people today. Anyone who thinks seriously about it realizes that progress is being made only on the scientific and technical levels, that is to say, on the purely material level. And not only does scientific progress not bring moral progress along with it, it can even be said to cause men to regress, for they have committed themselves to the exploration and exploitation of the physical world without taking any preliminary precautions.

It is important to know that there is a law by which a change in one area necessarily leads to changes in other areas. If you fail to take the necessary precautions, progress in one area will lead to regression in another. Men have attempted to put science in the place of religion, but in doing so they should have given science an added dimension by broadening its field of investigation. There has never been any reason why science and religion should not be the two sides of one reality; the one looking, as it were, to the outer world and the other to the inner world, for man lives simultaneously in both worlds. Of course, for this to be possible, men must be conscious that there are two sides to reality and must not give priority to one to the detriment of the other. In the course of the centuries, however, this is precisely what human beings have done: they have either rejected science in the name of religion, or they have rejected religion in the name of science. They have failed to understand that truth lay in their harmonious co-existence, for the universe is a whole.

You must understand that when I speak of scientific discoveries I am not thinking only of those that have been made within the last hundred years or so. It is true that there have been some gigantic transformations in our century, but all these things were already known a very long time ago. There have been civilizations in the past in which science was far more advanced than it is today and which were ultimately destroyed by it. And this is the danger that faces mankind today.

Human history does not follow a programme of smooth, continuous development. In the first place we have to realize that the world has already seen several human races whose development came to an abrupt end. Certain scientific or technical phenomena which were well known to them were lost or forgotten. I cannot go into details today; it is enough to mention that certain ancient civilizations knew that the earth was round and orbited round the sun, and then this knowledge was lost, and it was centuries before it was accepted again.

Today we are once again in a period of technical and scientific discovery, but however wonderful these discoveries may be, it is no good counting on them to achieve the lasting happiness of mankind. Even the most brilliant scientists will never find the meaning of life if they are content to explore only matter, for their field of research, their instruments, their laboratories and the objects they study are all external to themselves. There have been many brilliant scientists — some of whom were awarded the Nobel prize for their fantastic discoveries — who never resolved their own inner confusion. If they had known the philosophy of the initiates and learned to apply their methods, the scientific discoveries they made would have strengthened and enlightened them inwardly as well as outwardly. What a pitiful waste! What is the sense of discovering things that make life easier for everybody else and remaining in a permanent state of disarray oneself?

This is why I say to those who are engaged in scientific research: 'You are doing good work. Go on with your research, and God bless you! We need your discoveries, and you are producing many good things. But I warn you that however many discoveries you make, you will always be inwardly dissatisfied if you do not change your point of view.'

And the worst of it is that they lead the whole of society into error. In fact, it would be fair to say that it is scientists who prevent mankind from evolving, for in focusing all their attention on purely material and technical progress, they have completely neglected the question of psychic progress. They are not interested in ennobling men or improving their characters, but true progress is moral progress. This is the progress that the initiates are interested in, and it is because scientists neglect this that they will one day be seen as the enemies of true progress. Yes, their responsibility is immense, and they have failed to live up to it.

We really need to think about the value of all the technical triumphs of which scientists are so proud. Does true progress really consist in sending all kinds of contraptions to the other planets? What will be the end result of these expeditions? The exploitation of new resources and the introduction of the same disorders as those that exist on earth? Why do human beings have to disturb the whole universe? In itself, of course, there is nothing wrong in wanting to explore the universe, but there are a certain number of things that we should understand first. The trouble is that human beings respect nothing. Believing that they are the lords of creation they pillage and plunder, and it never occurs to them that one day they will have to pay for their brutal attitude. As long as scientists are only interested in doing violence to nature in order to discover and exploit its treasures, without a thought for the damage they are inflicting, they will never find the truth that initiates have discovered.

What must they do in order to find this truth? The reality that an initiate studies is the same reality as that studied by other men. But there is an essential difference in attitude, for an initiate is not content to limit himself to the physical world. He knows that there are three aspects or dimensions to every process in nature, the physical, the psychic and the spiritual, and he looks within to find the inner manifestations that correspond with those in the physical world. If scientists took the trouble to look more deeply into the laws that govern the universe, they would understand that all the different elements, objects and phenomena they study point to a vaster, richer world. It is because scientists do not understand how these laws work that scientific progress has not led to moral progress.

Take the question of waves, for example: when physicists discovered the existence of waves they should have pursued their investigations further. If they had, they would have seen that waves are not an isolated phenomenon; that they exist not only on the physical plane but also on the planes of thought and feeling. And once they had seen this they would never have been content with the discovery of the radio. They would also have found that the brain is an instrument that is capable of sending out and receiving waves, and would have seen that there was much to be done on that level, too. Today, of course, mental telepathy is recognized by a good many people, but not yet by all, and so far no one has discovered all the consequences it could have for the education and mastery of man's mental faculties. That is not all: once they discovered that waves did not recognize man-made boundaries, they should have started working immediately for the abolition of national boundaries, then their actions would have been in accord with what they had discovered. True, there has been some progress in this area, but it is still so slow.

So, as you see, scientists make all sorts of discoveries but they do not always understand the full significance of what they discover. Every scientific and technical discovery — the telephone, photography, recording techniques, radar, laser beams, and so forth — must be transposed on to the psychic and spiritual plane in order to be complete. This rule applies not only to the realm of physics but also to the discoveries of chemistry, astronomy, biology, and so on. Even in Mendeleyev's periodic table, for example, each element is the messenger of a subtler reality.

One day, when they are capable of seeing beyond the material dimension of reality, scientists will be in possession of true science. And this is a highly desirable state of affairs, for not only does true science bring knowledge and understanding, it is also a source of equilibrium, freedom and inner peace. Whereas, although no one can deny that contemporary science has given us all sorts of appliances and gadgets which make life easier, its narrow view of reality robs people of their freedom and often leaves them unhappier and less fit than before.

Contemporary science is still not true science. Scientists conduct their research without realizing that they have the basic ingredients of true science in their hands. Many of them are disappointed to see that technical progress does not change the world, and they wonder what they can do to contribute to the moral progress of mankind. Well, here is the answer to their question: while they work to discover the laws of the physical world, they must also work to discover the laws of the moral world.

Chapter Fourteen

SCIENTIFIC TRUTH

AND

THE TRUTH OF LIFE

If you wish to have a comprehensive idea of a building you must walk round it and look at it from all sides. In the same way, if you wish to have an accurate understanding of a situation you also have to 'walk round' it. Is this what most people do? No, instead of looking at a situation from all angles they cling to their own point of view, claiming vociferously that it is they who possess the truth; that it is they who have the right perspective. Unfortunately, as long as you confine yourself to one aspect of reality you will always be very far from the truth.

If you want to discover truth, you must never look at an isolated segment of time or space. If you reason on the basis of a short period of time, the duration of a human life for instance, you will never understand anything about the progression of events, for a life is only one link in a long sequence. You cannot understand what a person lives through in the course of one incarnation if you see it as an isolated experience; not only must you look at it in relation to all the incarnations that person has lived through in the course of hundreds and thousands of years, but you must also bear in mind that this sequence will continue into the future. It is impossible to understand the significance of the present if you do not see it as belonging to a continuum that includes past and future.

Everything that happens is a consequence of something that went before. This means that we cannot interpret today's events correctly unless we look at the past. It also means that we can work on the present (the result of the past) so as to shape a future that matches up to our hopes and desires. In order to understand a person's life therefore you must look at it not only as the consequence of a distant past but also as the starting point of a new life. You will never have a true appreciation of that life if you ignore the fact that it is inseparably linked to past and future lives. And this rule applies not only to the dimension of time, it also applies to the dimension of space. This means that scientists will never discover the whole truth about the things they study, whether they be inanimate objects or living beings, unless they fit them in to the overall context of life. Whatever their field of research, all scientists should think about this, for they all have a tendency to specialize.

The great merit of specialists is that they really do know their subject. Unfortunately, however, they rarely know anything about their neighbour's specialization. This is particularly striking in the field of medicine, where more and more doctors become specialists, and fewer and fewer become general practitioners. You will say that the specializations of doctors correspond to the specializations that we find in our own bodies, in which each organ (liver, lungs, heart, kidneys, and so on) has its own special function. True, but our specialists (our organs) are closely knit in a truly fraternal community in which all work together for the whole man.

No one can deny that specialization has made it possible to achieve fantastic progress in many areas. Scientists have to restrict the scope of their investigations if they want to go deeper into one particular field, but it is also very important that, having done this, they should be able to see the relationship between their own narrow field of study and creation as a whole. Is this what they do? No, they take a tiny piece of bark from the Tree of Life, and having measured, weighed and examined it in detail, they write books about it, and invite their students, colleagues and friends to listen to them lecturing about it. And this is what they call science. But by separating that little bit of bark from the tree they are separating it from the stream of universal life. To all intents and purposes it is dead. Not physically dead, perhaps, but dead insofar as the life of the cosmos is concerned.

One day, when scientists begin to understand this question more fully, they will realize with remorse that it is they who, because of their outlook and methods, have contributed enormously to a false under-standing of that vast whole that constitutes life. They cannot be faulted for cataloguing the characteristics of the minerals, plants or animals they study. What they say is true, everything is true... but that truth is only a fragment of a whole. To complete it they must restore the links that unite the object of their study with the vibrant, surging, radiant life of the cosmos. When minerals, plants and animals are cut off from this life they are deprived of what is essential to them. This means that as long as the specialists of different disciplines continue to work in the same way, the scientific truth they talk about will continue to be an incomplete, truncated truth.

Try to understand what I am saying. I am not criticizing or denying scientific discoveries. The problem lies elsewhere: in the minds of scientists; in their attitude towards life; in their inability to make the connection between their own particular branch of study and life as a whole. They attach too much importance to analysis and not enough to synthesis. What is worse, they are so used to using methods of dissection, segmentation and dislocation in their investigation of matter that they end by applying these same methods to the study of human beings. They think that human beings, too, can be understood if they are cut up into little bits. In fact this tendency to dissect everything, which is so much a part of scientific method, has become so widespread that it has led to all kinds of changes, even in the social, moral and spiritual life of mankind. Each individual man and woman wants to be separate and apart from others, and the result is hostility, rivalry and war. Yes, these are the fruits of analysis.

The same is true of countries and nations. Patriotism and nationalism are often no more than a manifestation of this universal philosophy of segmentation. I do not want to speak about any country in particular, for it is not my mission to meddle in politics. I simply observe what goes on and explain the principles involved in the light of initiatic science. In every country in the world, even in the West, separatist movements are springing up. Analysis is gaining ground all the time, and if this continues you will soon find that the whole world will be well and truly 'analysed'... Yes, chopped up in little bits! It is high time to introduce a little synthesis. I am not saying that countries should not be free and independent. I am simply saying that they should also be conscious of being members of one body, of a larger whole, for it is only in this way that the current of life can circulate harmoniously. Synthesis is life, eternity, immortality. I know that very few people will understand what I am saying, for mentalities have been distorted by all the theories popularized by newspapers, books and films, which constantly talk about uprooting, separating, getting rid of things.

Everybody is in favour of analysis; in favour, that is, of division, separation, dislocation, segmentation. Even in the family each member is so analytical that nobody can put up with anybody else, and families break up for the flimsiest reasons. I assure you, it is high time to study the question of synthesis, for synthesis is love, tolerance and understanding. Perhaps you will say that if synthesis is love, analysis must be wisdom. You are right, but, of course, this requires a good deal of elaboration.

On the symbolic level it is true to say that synthesis is love, because the heart adds and brings things together, whereas analysis is wisdom, because, on the contrary, the intellect subtracts, dissects and divides. However, we have to realize that not every synthesis is to be recommended any more than every analysis. We have to learn to juggle with these notions.

We could say, for instance, that there is more analysis than synthesis in the way some people love. Those who are content to love just one man or woman are analysts. They forget everybody else; they do not want to know them; they get no joy from knowing that they exist. And because they focus all their love on one person they inevitably meet with disappointment and suffering. Such people still have to learn the art of synthesis so as bring the whole world together in their love.

But let us get back to the question of science. It is because science confines itself to the world of facts that there is so much segmentation today. Nobody knows how to control the mountains of new information that become available every day; they are being smothered by it. I am not saying that scientists should stop studying and making new discoveries, I am simply saying that when they no longer know how to relate the facts they study to a greater whole, their vision of reality, far from becoming clearer, becomes more and more fragmentary and confused.

Nothing is more necessary than a central idea which serves as a guide to keep one on course, but as men of science have never understood this they keep piling everything up together in an unwieldy, overwhelming mass. You will say that science is content to study only what actually exists, and that we need to know about the habits of insects, microbes, bacilli and viruses, and how they spread, so as to defend ourselves against them. Well, I am not so sure about that. If human beings learned to live in synthesis, that is to say, in harmony, unity and love, they would be healthy, and it would not be so necessary to study all these little creatures, either in their bodies or in laboratories. Why is everything always being analysed - our blood, our urine, and goodness knows what else? We are so accustomed to being analysed that we cannot do without it any more. Learn to live in synthesis and you will not need any more analysis! You will perhaps know less about the composition of your urine, but you will not need that knowledge, because you will be healthy.

I realize, of course, that the work of many scientists obliges them to go beyond their own specialization and call on their colleagues in other branches. The construction of a satellite, for instance, requires the collaboration of several different disciplines, from mathematics to astrophysics; but although these methods may be adequate when it comes to building a machine, they are hopelessly inadequate when it comes to penetrating the secrets of life.

When people and things are cut off from universal life there is no way of knowing how life vibrates, pulsates, and manifests itself within them. A fruit must be studied while it is attached to the tree, otherwise it is impossible to understand that it is the culmination of the energies that flow through the tree. We are always hearing about the importance of 'scientific truth', but there is something more important than scientific truth, and that is the truth of life. To possess the truth of life is to be capable of linking each insignificant detail to a central governing idea; to see each element as part of the one great cosmic edifice, and in so doing to understand how each one participates in the life of the whole and vibrates in harmony with it. In this way, each fact that is studied separately finds its place as an element that contributes to the whole.

You must imitate scientists by observing and studying reality with attention and accuracy, but you must go further than they and learn to fit all the different elements together so that something that was not present in the separate elements begins to flow through them. And that something is life. True knowledge is found only in life. Separate the different elements and life is no longer there. It is not essential to be able to describe the shape, size or colour of a given element, or to list its properties, for as long as that element is taken in isolation it is cut off from life. But tie it in with all the other elements, and life appears. You can know all there is to know about the properties of the different elements, but if you do not know how life flows in and through them, you do not possess true knowledge.

Try to understand what I am saying. I am not saying that you must not specialize. I fully realize that in most cases this would be the equivalent of saying that you must not have a profession, for every profession is a specialization. I only mean that you must not allow your specialization to be at the centre of your preoccupations. It is life that must be at the centre of your preoccupations, life in the fullest and most elevated sense. Once you are firmly anchored to the one thing that is essential, you will be free to explore as many non-essentials as you wish.

It is impossible to have a proper philosophy of life unless you have clear ideas about the structure of the universe, the beings that inhabit it and the currents that flow through it. The first thing to study is man himself: what he represents, his place in the universe, the end for which he is destined and the factors within him which will enable him to attain that end. There is no reason why you should not also study crystallography, botany, zoology, astronomy and anything else you please. To the extent to which you have already worked at what is essential, all these other fields of science will be lit with a new light and reveal new dimensions.

The great failing of scientists is to believe that the methods they use in studying the physical world are universally valid and can be applied to every area of life, and as they have never seen God through their microscopes or telescopes, they say that he does not exist. Their studies and researches never cease to show them evidence of a sublime intelligence that governs the movement of the heavenly bodies, the passage of the seasons, the functioning of living organisms - plants, animals and human beings - but as they have never been in a position to argue the question face to face with their Creator, they deny that he exists and declare creation to be the work of chance. Well, let me tell these scientists that it is not in nature that there is a lack of intelligence but in their heads! They are incapable of reasoning and drawing the right

conclusions from their observations. They chop
the universe in bits and then proceed to reason
on the basis of the separate bits. This is why
they will never find the truth.

If you want to find the truth, you must rise
to a higher conception of life. This higher point
of view will not only enable you to reach a
fuller intellectual understanding of reality but
will set in motion a process of regeneration
deep within your being simply because you will
once again be united with the whole. You will
be in touch with the subtle currents of the
universe, immersed in the womb of cosmic life;
and as you share more fully in that life, in
communion with all creatures visible and
invisible, so will the scope of your
consciousness be enlarged.

This broader conception of science is also
true religion. What is the use of repeating that
the word religion comes from the Latin
religare, meaning to bind, if you spend your
time separating things? You will say that the
bond of religion is a bond with God. No doubt,
but what is the value of a bond with God if it is
accompanied by a separation from everything
else? The bond that links the Creator with his
creatures must also link all living creatures
with each other and with all the elements of
creation. True religion is the comprehension of
this bond. True religion therefore, implies true

science. The divorce between science and religion in which some people take so much pride is senseless. Those who separate science and religion are simply too narrow-minded; they understand neither the one nor the other. Is all this clear to you now?

Far from alienating us from God, the study of the physical world should bring us closer to him. This is why genuine initiates do not reject the world. For them it is a laboratory, and they make use of all the elements it contains, for they know that it is these elements that will enable them one day to produce the Philosophers' Stone. Those who want to sever all ties with the world are in error. God has endowed the world with unbelievable wealth, but we need the light of initiatic science to teach us how to use that wealth instead of being overwhelmed by it. The important thing is to possess this light in dealing with the world, not to cut ourselves off from the world. Those who cut themselves off from the world are signing their own death warrant.

It would be true to say that the methods used by initiates and scientists are complementary: scientists use an analytical approach, which enables them to study details, while initiates use a synthetic approach which embraces the whole. The ideal is to combine the two approaches. From now on, remember to find a place in the whole for everything you study, everything you see, hear or touch. Nothing must be left out; nothing must remain isolated, cut off from the Tree of Life. If you can achieve this attitude, if you have this unifying vision of reality, the subtle force-centres within you, which Hindu mystical tradition calls chakras, will gradually be awakened. Many methods of stimulating the chakras have been proposed, and some of them are very dangerous. The best way to awaken these centres - the only method I recommend - is to work to realize the unity of life within oneself.

Many initiates have appeared in the course of history, and they have not all manifested themselves in identical ways. Some have shown themselves to be primarily masters of love, others of purity, others of wisdom; but the vision of all genuine initiates eventually embraces the sum total of all things, all activities and all living creatures. All initiates have their own special mission, but no initiate is a 'specialist'. Each one strives to live life in all its fullness.

A master, or initiate, therefore, is someone who is concerned with the whole of life. He does not lose sight of the details, but for him it is life that takes priority over all else, and his concern is to protect, enrich and purify life, for this is the one reality which contains all others. The only way to lay hold on the fullness of life is to turn back to the Prime Cause, the Source, God himself. This is what you must do: take care to maintain your links with the Cause of all causes, the divine Source.

Chapter Fifteen

A FRESH VIEW OF REALITY

The reason why most human beings find life empty and monotonous is that their understanding of reality is too narrow and superficial. They base their opinion of people and things on appearances, and they think that they need to know nothing more to get along in life.

Let me give you the example of an attitude that is very common between men and women. When two people have known each other for a little while they have the impression that they have nothing more to learn about each other, and for this very reason they learn nothing new and begin to be bored and indifferent. Their relationship goes stale, and they drift apart and go their separate ways. It never occurs to them that the reason why their relationship has deteriorated is that they were blind to each other's subtler dimension, to their soul and spirit. And the worst thing about it is that they think that their behaviour shows them to be people of experience, sophisticated and unshockable, and that this will give them a certain prestige in the eyes of others. Well, their prestige will perhaps be enhanced in the eyes of those who are as blind as they are, but they are condemning themselves to a form of sclerosis, because they are cutting themselves off from the tide of life. People are alive; nature, too, is alive, and if you want to sense the presence of that life, certain faculties of perception within yourself must be refined and polished.

There are some very simple ways of doing this: for example, when you leave your house in the morning, look at the sky and the sun and try to imagine how you would feel if you were seeing them for the first time. In this way you will discover a subtle dimension of life that you had never noticed before because you have allowed an opaque screen to grow up within you. You will never understand things as they really are until you get rid of that screen.

True understanding is an ever-flowing spring; a perception that is constantly renewed and regenerated; a perpetual enchantment. And it is not enough to cultivate this attitude in relation to nature; you must also learn to cultivate it in relation to other human beings, for not only will it enable you to discover things you never dreamed of, but you yourself will become much more interesting and attractive to others.

The important thing is to partake of life, to be in communion with life. You can know all there is to know about the earth and the heavens; about minerals, plants, animals and the stars; about human beings, their languages and cultures, and their different ways of life... Yes, you can know all these things and still end by feeling dissatisfied and bored if you never learn to partake of the subtle currents of life that flow through them.

You will perhaps object that I am asking something very difficult of you, and that you do not know how to set about it. No, it is not difficult. The method I have just given you is very simple: you just have to try and look at people and things as though you had never seen them before. The advantage of this method is that it obliges you to be creators, and it is this ability to create that gives meaning to life. Have you never wondered how musicians and actors are capable of playing the same piece of music or acting in the same role over and over again, and still manage to have a powerful impact on their audience? It is because they are capable of playing or acting as though each performance were the first. All artists, even those who only perform the works of others, are creators, because they put life into each performance. Why should you not do as much? Why leave art to artists? At every moment you, too, can become creators by putting life into everything you do, everything you look at, everything you hear. The only condition is to do and look and hear as though it were for the first time.

This is a very great secret that I have given you today; very few people have ever discovered it or put it into practice. They live for years, doing everything more and more automatically. They eat and drink and move about, but always automatically, mechanically, and this is why they are never happy. You would be amazed if you knew how many things I have discovered by consciously applying this method of doing everything as though it were for the first time. In this way everything always seems new to me. And in reality, that is the truth: everything is always new. People and things are never the same from one day to the next, because they are alive, and those who are alive constantly radiate something new. Even metals vibrate differently from one day to the next. Even the necklaces, rings or watches that you wear every day change, and if you were sufficiently sensitive, you would perceive these changes in the movement of their electrons. The explanation is that these objects are always in touch with the ever-new currents of the cosmos, but as you do not feel anything, you think that they are always the same.

The fact is that nothing is ever the same, especially the sun. When the sun rises in the morning it is always new. Even an astronomer would tell you this. Seen from earth with the naked eye, the changes that take place in the sun are invisible, but astrophysicists have instruments that enable them to observe the life of the sun and to see the changing currents and radiations and eruptions. How could these changes in the sun fail to have repercussions throughout the whole solar system, amongst human beings, animals, plants, stones and even metals?

From now on, therefore, if you want to discover a truth that will give new meaning to your life, try to do everything as though it were for the first time. Every day when you wake up, think that today you are going to rediscover the world: that you are going to eat a slice of bread; look at the fire, or at water or a mountain; listen to some music; go and see your family or friends... all as though it were for the first time. If you do this, you will sense that your life becomes richer and more beautiful every day.

Chapter Sixteen

DREAMS AND REALITY

It is not what happens outside you that matters most. What is important is what goes on inside you. Reality is what you feel, what you experience.

We can find many examples in life which indicate that objective reality is less important than subjective reality. In the face of the same event, there will be people who rejoice, others who feel sad and others who will be angry. Also, there are a great many people whose lives are governed by impressions that have nothing to do with reality. Some live in anguish, believing themselves to be pursued by villains, who exist only in their minds, but who are so real to them that they can see them slinking behind a wall, creeping up on them, whispering amongst themselves. Others imagine that they only have to appear in public to awaken passionate devotion in every heart; every little gesture or smile on the part of others is seen as a manifestation of that passion; every word conceals a hidden meaning; even a show of indifference is interpreted as a declaration of love.

Yes, I could give you countless examples of people who live with a reality that they have invented for themselves. They rejoice or worry or get excited about things that do not exist or that they interpret in their own way, and however much one may try to show them that it is all an illusion, they refuse to be convinced. They keep returning to their phantasms. It is not objective reality that influences their subjectivity; it is their subjectivity that creates the illusion of an objective reality.

Such phenomena can be even more striking in dreams. You dream that you are falling over a cliff and are terrified, but then you wake and realize that the cause of your terror was not real, it was only a dream. And yet while you were dreaming you had not the slightest doubt that it was real. Some people say that while they are dreaming they are conscious that it is a dream, but this is very rare. Very few people are conscious of dreaming, and the emotions they experience are exactly what they would experience if the events they are dreaming about were real. And then when they wake, what a disappointment to find that they are no longer with their beloved, strolling hand-in-hand through a garden full of flowers and the song of birds. Or what a relief, on the contrary, to find that they are safely in bed and out of harm's way!

You will say that this is nothing new; that you have known all that for ages. Yes, I am quite sure you have, but have you ever used that knowledge to restore order to your inner life? Remember, knowledge is useful only if you can do something with what you know.

Observe your own reactions, and if you see that you tend to dramatize events and exaggerate their gravity, or, on the contrary, if you tend to minimize their importance or their beauty, try to adjust your point of view. Since our subjectivity continually reshapes objective reality, why should we not try to reshape it for the better?

Besides, who says that the waking reality you experience is true reality? Many initiates and sages teach that life is a dream and that one day we shall wake up and see that the world around us is illusory. This notion can be very helpful; you should try to work with it. When you are going through a difficult period, for example, tell yourself: I feel that I am suffering, or ill, or persecuted, but it is all an illusion; I am dreaming. When I wake up all this will have disappeared. Another way of looking at it would be to tell yourself: it is not I who am concerned by all these trials. They are happening to someone, but I do not know who... perhaps to my physical body? In any case they cannot touch the real me. I am out of reach of all that. I am a spectator. I am invulnerable.

You will say that in the meantime your sufferings will not be any the less. That is true. You are like someone in the grip of a nightmare which is so real to him that he cries out and sweats in anguish. Our feelings and emotions correspond to a certain reality, but they are not reality itself. Life is a dream; and since life is a dream, human beings are dreamers. The difference between an initiate and an ordinary human being is that an initiate knows how to use these notions of dream and reality. And you must learn to do the same. Tell yourselves that life is a dream and that true reality is what most human beings consider to be a dream, and try to live in that reality. Pause from time to time and concentrate on the world of light, beauty and purity, and picture yourself living in the midst of this marvellous world. It is a dream, to be sure, but why should this dream not be true reality? Besides, when you look on it as reality you are contributing to making it real. Try to do this and you will see that it will help you to make great progress.

Now, it is important to understand correctly what I have been saying, for there are different kinds of dreams. Every human being dreams, but most of their dreams are confused and coloured by greed. It is necessary to dream, but we must do so consciously, so that our dreams may be governed by knowledge and an upright intention. At the same time, we must not lose our grip on everyday life, however illusory it may be. To flee that reality under the pretext that it is an illusion is not the right solution either. We have to strike a balance between the sensation, on the one hand, that we are dreaming and, on the other, that what we are experiencing is reality. The fact that we are on this earth means that our work is here, but we still have to bear in mind that we are asleep, and that one day we shall wake up. Ordinary men and women think that an initiate is a visionary who believes in all sorts of unrealistic, impossible dreams, whereas they themselves are wide awake and eminently realistic. They do not realize that it is they who are asleep... and snoring! The ideal is to make our dreams coincide with true reality; with the reality that exists above and beyond appearances.

So try to remember this: do not take the sufferings and difficulties of life too seriously, otherwise they will defeat you, and life will become a burden to you. When difficulties arise, say to yourself: I cannot deny that this is happening; it is real; but it is not happening to me. I am an eternal, immortal spirit. This thought will give you greater courage and hope.

Chapter Seventeen

TRUTH TRANSCENDS

GOOD AND EVIL

In the minds of most men and women truth is the equivalent of good, and this means that they think that evil is not within the realm of truth. This is yet another question that has never been examined sufficiently closely. Truth is a medal, one face of which is good and the other evil. Of course, in the long run good must triumph, but it is no use thinking that we can achieve the triumph of good by eliminating evil.

The whole of life teaches us this. Take the example of how a human being is formed. The upper part of his body is designed for noble activities, such as seeing, hearing, thinking and speaking, whereas the lower part is engaged in the more vulgar functions of digestion and excretion. But both the noble and the vulgar activities are performed by the same human being, and if someone were to reject the latter on the pretext that they are not in good taste, he would die. One cannot separate the higher from the lower.

Our higher faculties draw energy from our lower functions. Man is like a tree: his lower functions are the roots that he needs in order to draw into himself nutritive elements, which he then transforms and distributes to the world around him in the form of flowers and fruit. Instead of always trying to rearrange the order established by divine wisdom, human beings should study it and try to understand it. If you embark on a campaign to uproot and destroy evil, you will be mutilating reality in exactly the same way as if you mutilated yourself by doing away with your digestive and sexual organs.

Or take the example of the circulatory system. Our blood is an intermediary between the air we breathe and the cells of our body. How does nature cleanse blood that has become charged with impurities? Does it have to be removed from our bodies and replaced by clean blood? No, it is the oxygen in our lungs that purifies it. Nature has found a way of transforming an evil within us into good. And when you think of how the forces of nature have been domesticated over the course of the centuries, you see that man can also transform an evil into good: wind has been harnessed to turn the wheels that grind flour; waterfalls are used to produce electricity, and so on. I am not saying that those who take up arms against evil are not to be commended for their enthusiasm, their spirit of sacrifice and their love of God, but we still have to recognize that their zeal is misplaced. Whatever we do, there is no getting away from the two-fold nature of reality — good and evil, light and darkness, life and death — and we must know that neither one will ever vanquish the other. Of course, when I say this I am talking about the conditions we experience on earth. If you manage to rise to the divine world, you will find other conditions, but in the meantime you are on earth, and the wisest course is to study and understand the meaning both of the evil that manifests itself in your life — illness, difficulties and enemies — and of your own weaknesses.

Truth does not reside in evil, to be sure, but it is not to be found exclusively in good either; it is in good and evil at the same time, or, rather, it is in a principle which transcends both and is capable of working with both. If you never try to go beyond appearances and find this higher principle that governs both good and evil, you will never understand their relationship or the interplay, the duels, that go on between them. Good and evil are actors on the stage of life. If evil did not exist to spur good on to action, good might go to sleep and never accomplish anything.

Good is the one thing all human beings wish for with all their might, but as they are rarely in agreement about what it is, all their contradictory concepts end by producing evil. This is the cruel reality: each individual is so bent on ensuring the triumph of his own 'good' — which is never the good of others — that the inevitable result is evil. Even when, as sometimes happens, the longed-for good actually materializes, people soon tire of it. Sometimes they tire of life itself as well. Why? Because life is too comfortable. Evil forgets about them, and to be forgotten and neglected by evil is not as marvellous as it sounds.

Life is a drama in which evil plays a key role: it is the character that upsets the settled order and makes things happen, that makes a play into a comedy, a tragedy or a drama. As the curtain goes up we see the uneventful life of a group of people. Then a stranger arrives on the scene, and out of ambition, love, pride, greed, jealousy or stupidity, precipitates a crisis in their lives. All concerned are in a turmoil and have to struggle to survive and find a solution to the resulting chaos. By the end of the play some of the characters are dead, others have fallen ill or gone mad, and others have learned wisdom by using the difficulties of the situation. There would be no play, no drama, if there were no disruptive element to make things happen. We might even say that without evil life itself would make no progress.

These explanations will probably not satisfy philosophers or theologians, who have very complicated theories about good and evil. But complicated theories do nothing to solve the problem of evil. You can only solve the problem of evil by action, by learning to transform it; otherwise it becomes stronger by feeding on your ignorance and weakness. Truth, therefore, is not the same thing as good; or, rather, it is the good of those who have learned to transform evil.

You will gain victory over evil not by exterminating your enemies, but by transforming your enemies into friends. In this way, instead of being surrounded by people whose one idea is to injure you, you will be surrounded by friends who think only of helping you. This is difficult to achieve, of course. It is very easy to kill someone by putting a bullet through him, poisoning his drink, planting a bomb or turning on the gas and blowing up his house. It is far more difficult to work on yourself and on him so that he becomes your friend, but it is well worth making the effort, and in doing so you prove that you live by the truth.

Only the great initiates really understand the question of evil. They are not content to know and work with good; they also explore the domain of evil. This is why some initiates, like Jesus, are said to have descended into hell. Of course, before doing this they take the necessary precautions and make sure that they are well armed, and once their protection is assured, they descend to explore the regions of hell and its inhabitants. The dictum, 'Know, will, dare and hold your peace,' was addressed to such as these, and as I have told you before, the most mysterious of these injunctions is to 'dare'. Why? Because to dare means to brave the powers of hell in order to see, understand, know and conquer. And those who have ventured into hell must hold their peace, for one must never speak of hell to those who are unprepared.

You will probably say that you have never heard anyone speak of hell as a region whose inhabitants could be studied. I know, but it is high time that you put aside the fanciful descriptions of hell that you have heard and began to have more realistic notions about it. What is hell? It is the cesspool of the universe, and as such it plays a necessary and very useful role in ridding the world of its refuse. In it are collected all that is vicious and corrupt. The notion is easy to understand. Look at what human beings do: do they live in the midst of filth and refuse? No, they put it in bins or bags and dispose of it in a pit or an incinerator. And if human beings have found ways of disposing of their refuse, is it not reasonable to suppose that cosmic intelligence also has a solution? Yes, the solution chosen by cosmic intelligence is the place that Christians call hell. Hell is the dumping ground for all the refuse of the universe. But there is one important thing you must know, and that is that the great spirits of the higher world come and collect all this refuse and use it to create wonderful things. So hell is a kind of warehouse and laboratory also, for nature never discards anything as useless; she sends it to what we would call a purification plant, and once it is cleansed of its impurities it is recycled and used for new creations.

Even hell is useful therefore. Even hell contributes to the economic order of the cosmos. I know that many priests and theologians will not agree. They are persuaded that hell is full of the damned who are condemned to burn and suffer torture for all eternity. Well, this is false. We know that it is false, firstly, because such a belief is diametrically opposed to the love of God: God can never cast off one of his creatures for all eternity. It is also incompatible with the wisdom of God; for God is wise, he does not let anything go to waste. Everything in creation is useful, and everything is used, but only after it has been cleansed and transformed.

All impure elements are swept up by the forces of the psychic plane and consigned to hell, from which other forces, other spirits, collect them and then transform them. From the flanks of hell flow streams and rivers of pure energy, for contrary to popular belief, hell is not a sealed dungeon from which nothing can ever escape. There are all kinds of ducts and channels through which the newly-transformed elements flow back to the world. Does this astonish you? There is really nothing to be astonished about. Hell is not a dead end, a blind alley that leads nowhere. The currents of evil flow back through certain channels to nourish, irrigate and fertilize other, unknown regions.

People think that the impure elements that accumulate and stagnate in the place they call hell are always the same. Not at all. New loads of refuse are constantly arriving to replace those that have already been taken away and processed. The spirits of light cannot tolerate anything that does not vibrate in unison with the cosmos. This is why discordant elements are cast into what is traditionally known as 'outer darkness'. And 'outer darkness' is hell: a place that is cut off from divine light, but from which the re-cycled elements are put back into circulation in the life of the cosmos.

I do not want to discuss the reasons why the Church has failed to explain the truth about hell to the faithful, but anyone who inquires into initiatic science will inevitably encounter the question, and will have to study it and understand the truth of it in order to advance. The notion of hell that the Church has given the faithful has not really helped them to transform themselves. For centuries they went in fear of hell, but is fear a good tutor? I do not think so. Besides, the time always comes when people cease to fear, and then they scoff at the things they once believed and tell jokes about them. I am sure that you all know funny stories about hell. I remember some that were popular in my youth in Bulgaria. This one, for instance. An old Turk says to his son:

'Listen Ali, you must stop drinking, otherwise you will go to hell, and they will punish you by hanging a barrel round your neck.'

'Oh,' exclaims Ali, with sudden interest, 'will the barrel be full?'

Then there are those who are always cold, and joke that in hell, at least, they will be warm. No, the threat of hell does not make much impression on anybody any more.

There is also the story of the Orthodox bishop who was dying, and who bade farewell to his wife saying: 'I will meet you in heaven.' Being a man of righteousness — in his own opinion at least — he was sure that his place was in heaven. He was less sure about his wife, but still... she was his wife and her years by his side had surely sanctified her! A few years later his wife died and went to heaven, where she began to look for her husband. In spite of all her inquiries, nobody seemed to have heard of him. Finally, she went and asked St Peter where she could find her husband.

'My good woman,' said St Peter, after consulting his big book, 'There is no one of that name in heaven. Let me look in Purgatory.' But he was not in Purgatory either. There was only one possibility left: could he be in hell?

'Impossible!' cried his devoted wife, 'Not my dear husband!' But that, alas, is where St Peter's register showed him to be... he showed her the page with his name on it.

'Ah, then that is where I must go.' said she, 'We promised to meet again when I died.' St Peter tried to explain that the other world was not like the earth; you could not just go and drop in on people who were in another section, but she cried so much and made such a fuss that finally he relented and gave her a pass. In hell she began searching and making inquiries all over again, and suddenly she saw him. He was up to his neck in a huge cauldron of boiling liquid.

'Oh my poor husband! And to think that I expected to find you in heaven... How unhappy you must be!'

'Oh, it is not too bad.' said he, 'In fact I am in a privileged position. I am standing on the shoulders of the cardinal!' What a commentary on how seriously Christians take the notion of hell!

In conclusion, never forget that there are always two sides to truth: the pure and the impure; the light and the dark; good and evil, and true knowledge must include both. Of course, if you are vulnerable and ignorant it is better not to set out to explore hell. If I talk about it, it is not in order to encourage you to go there. I am simply trying to explain how it is that the greatest initiates are those who are capable of confronting hell, for it is in doing so that they come to possess all knowledge.

Chapter Eighteen

'THE TRUTH SHALL MAKE YOU FREE'

I

You still do not fully realize what blessings truth can bring you. You think that you can get along very well without it. Yes, you can live without truth, but without truth you cannot be free. Only truth can make you free. It was Jesus who said, 'The truth shall make you free.' And what is more desirable than to be free?

Every quality or virtue has its own particular properties: the property of love is to impart warmth; the property of wisdom is to impart light, and the property of truth is to give us freedom, because freedom has a special link with the will and with strength. As we have already seen, however, there are different degrees or levels in the manifestations of truth, and our freedom depends on the level on which we stand.

Perhaps some illustrations taken from nature will help you to understand this more clearly. Moles live underground, far from the light, and when they want to move they have to dig long tunnels in the ground, and their tunnels are often destroyed by a passing plough. Their life in dark, narrow tunnels probably suits them because they are moles; they can imagine no other. The life of a fish is freer than that of a mole; the environment in which fish live and move is lighter and much more spacious. But the life of birds is freer still: the wide open spaces are theirs to fly about in; they are free to sing and rejoice in the light of the sun. Moles, fish and birds are symbols which correspond to different levels of consciousness, and it is the level of consciousness that determines destiny.

And now let us take the image of a tree. A tree has roots, a trunk and branches, and the branches bear leaves, flowers and fruit. The roots of a tree live deep underground in total darkness and work to absorb the nutrients from the soil to produce the raw sap, which then rises through the trunk. Cut off as they are from light and air, roots have an arduous, thankless task and know only obstacles, difficulties and constraints. The trunk, on the other hand, rises heavenwards, bearing currents of intense life: at the core are the upward channels carrying the raw sap to the leaves, while the cell sap flows down through channels lying along the outer edge of the trunk. Little by little, as the trunk grows taller and stronger, it acquires new branches which are free to sway joyfully in the light and air and to display the life and beauty of their leaves, flowers and fruit.

The roots of a tree absorb elements from the earth; its leaves absorb light from the sun which transforms the raw sap into the vital cell sap; colourful, scented flowers prepare to become fruit, and the fruit not only provides nourishment for men and beasts, it also contains the seeds from which other trees will be born. Roots, trunk and branches are all useful and beautiful in their own way; but would we not all prefer to live amongst the leaves, flowers and fruit in the branches of a tree which are open to the light and warmth of the sun?

The universe is like a tree. In fact, in many religious traditions the cosmic tree is a symbol of the universe. Depending on the stage they have reached in their evolution and their progress on the path of truth, human beings dwell either in the roots, the trunk or the branches of the cosmic tree. Those who live in the roots are crushed by their conditions; the constraints that weigh on them and the darkness that surrounds them make it impossible for them to do anything to change their own destiny, and even the most exalted spirits are powerless to help or instruct them, for they are incapable of understanding what they hear. It is not — as certain religions would have us believe — that such degenerate beings are cast into outer darkness. No, they are not cut off from truth, for truth embraces the whole of creation. But there are reasons why these beings, who have never managed to free themselves from the truth of moles and roots, have been placed in conditions where it is very difficult for them to evolve.

Those who live in the trunk of the cosmic tree enjoy greater freedom, for there is more light in the trunk than in the roots. But even here the light is not sufficient to reveal all truth to them. They still have to rise to the level of the leaves, flowers and fruit. Only there can they truly possess light and freedom.

The function of the roots corresponds to that of the stomach: both absorb nourishment. Those human beings for whom truth is confined to the need for food and drink — which symbolize all our needs on the physical plane — dwell in the stomach, or roots. And although the satisfaction of these needs affords them a certain amount of pleasure, it is not surprising that they often feel hemmed in or crushed by circumstances.

A similar parallel can be drawn between the trunk of a tree and the chest or upper part of our bodies, within which are the heart and lungs. The function of these two organs is analogous to the function of the tree trunk, in which the raw sap is transformed into cell sap; for the heart sends impure blood to be purified by the oxygen in the lungs, from where it goes on to nourish the whole body. Like the raw sap, the blood charged with impurities flows upwards, and, like the cell sap, the purified blood flows downwards. The thorax, containing the heart and lungs, corresponds to the astral plane of feelings and emotions, and those who dwell in this region are subject to fluctuating moods.

The branches of a tree, with the leaves, flowers and fruit, correspond to the head. Those who live in the head, that is to say, on the mental plane, are freer and more enlightened; above all, their creative potential is far greater.

These three stages of evolution correspond to the three principles that make up the human psyche: the intellect, the heart and the will. The intellect needs light; the heart needs joy and spaciousness; the will needs freedom in which to act. Obviously, light, spaciousness and freedom are not to be found in the roots. Light, joy and freedom truly exist only in the topmost branches of the cosmic tree.

Our freedom depends therefore on our degree of evolution. This means that for a human being, just as for any other creature, there can be no such thing as absolute freedom. Only God the Creator is truly free. Even the angels and archangels, even the cherubim and the seraphim are not absolutely free. All created beings are dependent on their Creator, and their degree of freedom is proportionate to their position in the immense hierarchy of beings in the universe.

And now let me take some examples from the cosmos. Astronomy distinguishes many different types of heavenly bodies, amongst which are comets, planets and suns. A comet, dashing through space and looking like a dishevelled head of hair, approaches the sun, saying, 'I have found truth; I have found my master!' But it does not stay close to the sun for long; just long enough to receive a little of the sun's warmth before it dashes off again to repeat the same scenario of finding and then abandoning another sun.

Planets behave quite differently: revolving faithfully round the sun, they receive in return a constant flow of warmth and light. But they also rotate on their own axis, and this means that they are subject to the alternation of day and night, heat and cold: when one side is lit the other is in darkness. However, nothing prevents them from pursuing their patient course around the sun.

As for suns, they are inexhaustible sources of light and heat which distribute their treasures to all creatures.

Comets, planets and suns can also be found amongst human beings. The comets are those who wander through life with no fixed spiritual abode and no ideal; those who lead a chaotic, rudderless existence. The planets are those who gravitate round a centre. They have their ups and downs, but they are faithful to their chosen path, for they sense that they must never stray from the spiritual ideal which is their source of light and warmth. Finally there are the suns: these are the great masters and initiates who have reached such heights on the path of love and wisdom that nothing can make them deviate or separate them from their ideal. They are always at the centre, and from there they give light and warmth to the creatures around them.

Moles, fish and birds; roots, trunks and branches; comets, planets and suns... all these examples from nature denote three categories of beings, and each category has its own laws: the first is ruled by the law of necessity; the second by the law of free will, and the third by the law of divine providence.

The law of necessity governs primitive beings who, in one incarnation after another, persist in seeking only the satisfaction of their most brutish needs. They are so firmly entrenched in matter that they have no freedom of movement, no possibility of choosing any alternative to the conditions they have been given. Their path is a hard one and they are obliged to follow it.

The law of free will governs those who are more highly evolved, those whose attitudes and actions in previous incarnations give them a certain freedom of choice today. To be sure, this freedom has its limits, but at least they have a choice between two possibilities. The disciples of all spiritual teachings, artists, scientists and philosophers — in short, all those who want to grow and advance — belong to this category.

Finally we come to the law of divine providence, the law which governs the great masters and initiates. Many paths are open to them, and they are free to choose between them. Life lies open before them, bright and glorious, because they are suns, and light dwells within them.

Comets are symbols of those men and women who are ruled by the law of necessity, under which they have no freedom of choice. They are perennial victims, victims of their

own blindness and their own lower instincts.
Try as we might to help them, there is no way
of releasing them from their fate. It is good to
try to help them, in the hope of igniting some
small spark of light within them, but it is no
good deluding oneself. The poor wretches still
have much suffering and many bitter blows to
endure from the hands of fate before they can
extricate themselves from their appalling
conditions.

Those who correspond to the planets, on
the other hand, are governed by the law of free
will, and it is within their power to make
constant progress on the path of righteousness.
Their route is strewn with difficulties and
obstacles of all kinds, but if they stumble they
are capable of picking themselves up again.
When faced with two possible choices they
must be very attentive to the inner voice that
guides them, for if they make a wrong decision,
they will have to endure the consequences to
the bitter end. If you are on the roof and want
to get down to the garden, you can choose to
jump to the ground or to climb down a ladder.
If you jump you will immediately be subject to
the law of gravity and are likely to fall heavily
to the ground. You are free only until you
actually leap over the edge; from then on it is
too late, you are bound to fall. Of course, if you
do choose the wrong solution, you are free to

pick yourself up again, but at the price of what pain and effort!

The life of a sun is ruled by the law of divine providence. The suns are free; they can choose to follow paths yet unknown to the great majority of human beings. In the three-dimensional world in which we live we are free to move from side to side, up and down, forwards and backwards. But in the worlds of four or five dimensions, or more, in which the spirits of these great beings live, the choices are infinite. Such beings are free because the supreme freedom of God abides and manifests itself in them.

Only the pure, divine spark of the spirit within us is free. To attain some measure of real freedom therefore we must identify with our spirit, and gradually, as this identification becomes effective, we shall become stronger and better able to extricate ourselves from our circumstances.

To use a different metaphor, we could say that to identify with the spirit is to rise above the clouds. As long as there are clouds over your head, you are at their mercy; if you want to see the sun, you have to wait until they obligingly move out of the way, and while waiting for them to move, you have to endure the cold and dark, fog and rain. And as you do not realize that it is you who created this situation for yourself, you complain that the sun is hiding from you, that God has forsaken you. But this is not true. You have this impression because you yourself have chosen to remain below cloud level. If you learned to raise your consciousness and keep it above the level of the clouds, you would immediately find the sun. The sun is always shining on the other side of the blanket of clouds.

Those who are ruled by the law of necessity are not only below cloud level. Like moles and worms, whose mission it is to prepare the ground for those who will come after them, they live underground. On the surface of the earth live those who are subject to the laws of free choice but who are still dependent on the goodwill of the clouds. Whereas those who are subject to the law of divine providence are always above the clouds, where the skies are always clear and the light of the sun, symbolically speaking, always shines on them.

Most human beings live below the clouds, where life is sometimes very difficult. But one should not complain about these difficulties. Complaints are useless; they have never helped to make life easier. The only way to change things is to cultivate an attitude of openness and cheerful acceptance. If you are discontented and disgruntled, you will only become tense, and if you are tense you will never succeed in improving your situation. On the contrary, you will find yourself sliding back into the realm of necessity. Your options will become fewer, your path will become narrower; even the tissues of your body will lose their flexibility. If your attitude is always negative, you will never be able to improve your situation; it will only improve if and when you adopt the right attitude.

There is no law that condemns someone to be a perpetual victim of fate. Blind fate exists only for those who sever their ties with the spirit. However bad the situation may be you can always remind yourself that you are a spirit and that you have the power to change your destiny. Of course, you will be able to change only a very small proportion of your situation — perhaps one per cent — to begin with. But if you continue to work in the right direction, you will eventually put a whole solar system between yourself and fate. The important thing is to be capable of changing direction. As soon as you realize that you are going the wrong way you must turn round and start walking the other way, and one day your destiny will be completely transformed.

A disciple has a clear understanding of the laws of destiny. He knows that the ordeals he is called on to endure in this life are the consequence of his transgressions in previous incarnations. The time has come for him to pay his debts, to make reparation and learn from his mistakes, and in order to do this he has to accept all the conditions imposed by divine justice. Nothing can hinder or prevent the decisions of divine justice from being realized. If you are meant to meet with failure, or to fall ill, or to get entangled in a disastrous relationship, there is nothing you can do to escape it. On the physical plane you are not free. If you want to be free you must rise to the spiritual plane. Through prayer and meditation you can link yourself to the divine world, and work to increase your inner light, strength, purity and love. Thanks to these virtues, you will be in a position to transform your trials, but not to avoid them.

Suppose someone were to get it into his head that he can take up arms against the winter and prevent it from coming. In the long run he would be obliged to admit that winter is stronger than he is and that he is going to have to put up with it. Well, this is how most people behave in relation to the events of life: they think that they are strong enough to prevent them... and they end by falling victim to them! But a disciple is well aware that winter must come one day, so he prepares for it by getting in a good supply of wood and coal and warm clothes. Then when it comes he can welcome it without fear... and both the disciple and the winter are content! The problem of how to deal with the trials ordained by destiny can be solved, therefore, but the solution is not to oppose them but to stock up on food and fuel and warm clothes; that is to say, to grow in wisdom and love so that when difficulties come we can face up to them with lucidity and courage. This is where our power and freedom lie.

If you have come into the world with many debts still to pay, you must work hard and earn as much as possible before disaster strikes, so that when it does you will be given the help you need. You may be able to escape a particular ordeal when it first confronts you, but if you run away, you must realize that it will catch up with you again a few years later, or in a future incarnation; and when it comes back for the second time it will be twice as severe. And who knows whether you will have the conditions you need to face up to it then? It is much better to try to pay off all your debts at once in your present incarnation.

How can you do this? Well, the best way to pay your debts is to put yourself in the service of the Lord and work for the coming of his kingdom. When you work unselfishly for the good of mankind you share the wealth of the Universal White Brotherhood on high. In other words, your brothers and sisters in the divine world begin to share the burden of your debts; they help you to bear your sufferings. There is one thing you must understand, however, and that is that all this takes place on the plane of consciousness, not on the physical plane. It is not on the material plane that you will be helped; it is on the spiritual plane. Work for the kingdom of God, therefore! If you work for yourself alone you will have to suffer whatever destiny is in store for you.

II

It would be true to say that from the day they are born human beings set out on the quest for truth. A tiny child only a few months old is already busy exploring the world. His eyes and ears notice all that goes on around him. Everything he can lay his hands on is tested by being put into his mouth. As soon as he can talk he asks endless streams of questions. Later he goes to school and is instructed in many subjects. Finally, after years and years of schooling, he feels the need to be free and independent. In his earlier years his parents and teachers were the models he respected and looked up to, but now he rejects them and decides to rely only on himself. Henceforth, he will find his own truth by pursuing his own experience.

All this is normal and good, but how is it that when people say they want to experience life for themselves it usually means that they want to experience dangerous things, such as sexual promiscuity or the use of alcohol or drugs? Why does the desire to experience things for oneself never mean the desire to explore the path of light and the divine virtues?

Everybody wants to get out of the rut of everyday life and taste something new and original, but it is the spiritual life that offers the widest range of new experiences. In their eagerness to taste every possible experience, why does nobody include the experience of prayer and meditation? Why do they never try to make contact with the world of light? Why do they never attempt to tread the path of love and wisdom, under the guidance of the initiates and great masters? I have no quarrel with the fact that at some point young people want to break free from the influence of their parents and educators, but this does not justify their rushing headlong into all kinds of rash ventures with only their thirst for independence to guide them.

Those who decide to ignore the experience of their elders show a misguided spirit of independence. In any case, whether they admit it or not, they cannot ignore that experience entirely. What do novelists, poets, philosophers

and painters do? Each one lives his life in his
own way, and the works they create inevitably
reflect the way they live. When they leave this
world, their works are bequeathed to other men
and women, who find nourishment and
inspiration in them. In this way a heritage of
ideas and sentiments gradually grows up over
the centuries and becomes the property of each
one of us, almost, one might say, from the day
of our birth. This means that in reality we are
all immersed in the lives of others. We cannot
avoid being influenced by their thoughts and
feelings, their discoveries and their awe and
wonder, but also by their errors and anxieties.
So, when we talk about being free, what
exactly are we talking about? It is not possible
to live without being influenced by others.

Influence is a law of life. We are constantly
influenced by all that we see and hear, and taste
and touch, by all that we eat and breathe.
People often think that they are acting
completely freely simply because they do not
know what it is that is influencing them. As a
matter of fact, it is just as well that they do not
always know, for if they knew that they were
acting under a good influence, their absurd
thirst for independence might well lead them to
reject it!

If you seriously want to find salvation, you
must understand how important it is to be

guided by the world's great spirits, past and present. Their experience is so much richer than ours, and they have solved so many of life's problems that they are like living books, able and willing to communicate to us all that precious knowledge. When we accept their guidance we continue to live and act and experience things for ourselves, but they are there to help us, and our experience is enriched by a higher element that comes from them.

In rejecting all spiritual and moral authority and obeying only their own inclinations, human beings are simply reproducing the first fault of Adam and Eve. Genesis tells us that God placed Adam and Eve in the Garden of Eden and forbade them to eat the fruit of the Tree of the Knowledge of Good and Evil. When they disobeyed they were expelled from the Garden.

The mystery that has always surrounded the Tree of the Knowledge of Good and Evil concerns the forces that are active in nature. Man occupies a specific position in nature, and with that position goes a corresponding level of consciousness which does not allow him to know or experience all that exists. It may be true to say that curiosity is one of the most powerful forces for human evolution, but there are certain experiences for which human beings are still not ready, and to embark on the exploration of them prematurely is to expose oneself to great dangers. I have already talked to you at length about the Tree of the Knowledge of Good and Evil.[1] Before the Fall, the first human beings lived, symbolically speaking, amongst the flowers of the cosmic tree, but when they sought to broaden their field of investigation they descended into the roots. There is ample scope for exploration amongst the roots, to be sure, but in discovering this they also discovered limitation and death.

There is only one way to re-conquer our freedom, and that is to turn back and start on the upward path again. How can we do this? By doing the will of our Creator. There can be no freedom except in submission to God, whom the psalmists call the Most-High, who is all power, all wisdom and all love. By setting themselves apart from the Creator, whether consciously or unconsciously, human beings become the slaves of inferior entities who have something to gain from seducing and dominating them, just as the serpent seduced Adam and Eve, and caused them to be driven from paradise. The serpent depicted in Genesis symbolizes a whole category of malevolent beings who, having rebelled against God, seek

---

1 See *The Tree of the Knowledge of Good and Evil*, Izvor Collection, No. 210.

to drag men down and persuade them to join them in their rebellion. This is why, if we now want to regain our freedom, we must renew our bonds with the luminous entities that have remained loyal to the Lord.

The word 'freedom' acquires its full significance only on the highest plane, on the plane of God himself. God manifests himself in us, and it is because he is free and because he is within us that we, too, feel free: we are free with his freedom. God acts within us. We are alive because we live by the free action of God.

Those who seek freedom by abandoning their responsibilities or following the dictates of their passions and lower instincts become slaves to the ignoble entities to whom they open their doors. If the Lord is not your guest, you will be invaded by demons. If you do not ask God to dwell within you and fill your soul and spirit with his own strength and light and freedom, the empty space within you will be occupied by your enemies. All the anguish and distress of human beings come from the fact that they are inhabited by enemies.

You will never find freedom if you continue as you are, because you are not looking for it in the right place or the right form. There are people who say, 'I am not going to tie myself down to a job or a wife or children. No obligations for me. I intend to be free!' But do you really think that such people are free? No, inwardly they are even less free than others, because their desire for freedom is not motivated by a noble, altruistic ideal.

'The truth shall make you free,' said Jesus. The truth that makes us free is the truth of love and wisdom; the truth of the initiates. This is the thought expressed in Master Peter Deunov's song, *Kaji mi ti istinata*, in which the disciple says, 'Tell me the truth that gives freedom to my soul,' and the Master replies, 'Be conscious, love, sow, build and give all.'

Truth, therefore, can never be a servitude. It is because most human beings still do not understand that truth is the fruit of wisdom and love that they seek to enslave others in the name of their own truth. People who try to subjugate others in this way must learn that they are not serving truth, for in violence there is neither love nor wisdom. You say, 'But if some people refuse to accept the truth, surely they must be forced to do so.' No, the truth must never be forced on anyone. Besides, it would do no good if it were. You must realize that there are many people who are incapable of accepting the truth, because they are still alienated from love and wisdom, and heaven forbids us to try to force it on them. This is why I say that the teachings of the great masters are for those who are already prepared;

for those who have acquired a certain amount of experience and have understood that true life lies in spiritual growth. I am sorry to say that those who have not yet understood this will have to wait until life has beaten them into shape with its great hammers.

The hammers of a genuine master are very small. He cannot use them to rough-hew great blocks of granite; he reserves his tools for other, more delicate works of art. When he sees a face that has already been shaped and prepared he knows that he can do something with it. With a few little taps of the hammer he seeks to refine the details and make it more harmonious and expressive, so as to bring out in each human face the original lines of the visage of God.

We must seek freedom within the framework of submission to God. Jesus expressed magnificently the full meaning of this submission when he said, in the Lord's Prayer, 'Hallowed be thy name, thy kingdom come, thy will be done in earth as it is in heaven.' At another time he said, 'I have come to do the will of him who sent me.' If we, too, want to attain the realm of divine providence, then we, too, must become workers in the vineyards of the Lord. In this way, when our creditors — the laws of the spiritual world that we have transgressed — threaten to punish us for our unpaid debts by dragging us off to prison, the Lord himself will intervene:

'Leave him alone, he is my servant.'

'Yes, but he is in our debt.'

'What for? How much does he owe you?'

'He committed such and such a sin and broke such and such a law.'

'Very well, his debts will be paid, but he is working for me, so it is I who will pay them.'

God is just. He does not drive away honest creditors. He says, 'I will pay you what he owes. Take it and be glad.'

This is why it is to our advantage to work for the Lord. We all have countless debtors, and to pay them all off we would need an immense fortune, which cannot be earned easily or rapidly. When the Lord sees that all our thoughts, and all our work and love are dedicated to him, he pays our debts for us.

It is no use telling your creditors that you belong to a very distinguished family or that you are very learned. They are not interested in that; they are only interested in being paid, and as long as we still have unpaid debts we shall continue to feel them twitching and tugging in our hearts and our heads. When we dwell in truth we shall no longer be dunned by creditors. If they still come and badger us today, it is because we are still in the trunk of the tree and still have to suffer certain constraints. In order to regain our freedom, we must climb back to the top of the tree.

The *Tales from the Arabian Nights* has a story that is very interesting from the point of view of initiatic science. It is said that King Solomon possessed magical powers which enabled him to command the spirits of nature, and he used these powers to send spirits into the bowels of the earth or the depths of the oceans to find and bring back the precious materials he needed to build the temple of Jerusalem. Whether this is true or not I really could not say. In any case, it makes no difference to the lesson to be drawn from the story...

One day a very powerful spirit refused to submit to Solomon's commands and the king punished him by shutting him up in a bottle, which he sealed with his seal before throwing it into the sea. During the first hundred years of his imprisonment the genie swore that if someone came to deliver him he would make him very rich. But no one came. During the second hundred years he swore that he would give his deliverer all the treasures of the earth. But no one came. During the third hundred years he swore that he would make his deliverer a powerful monarch. But still no one came. At last, as the centuries rolled by, the genie became more and more desperate and angry, and swore that if anyone should deliver him he would slay him without mercy.

Eventually, after much journeying to and fro on the bottom of the sea, the bottle with the genie in it was washed up on the shore near to the home of a poor fisherman. Every day this man would cast his nets into the water, but he never caught more than a few fish, just enough to eke out a miserable existence with his wife and children. Then one morning, when he hauled in his net, he felt that there was something heavy in it. 'Perhaps I have caught a really big fish,' thought he joyfully, and his disappointment was great when he found that it was not a fish, but a copper bottle sealed with an embossed leaden seal. To begin with, he looked at it with disgust, but then it occurred to him that if someone had taken such pains to seal it up in such a way, it must contain something valuable, and taking his knife he prized open the seal. His first impression was that the vessel was empty, but gradually, as he stood and looked at it, a thread of smoke began to emerge from it, which grew and grew until it was so huge that it stretched far out to sea and hid the sun behind a thick black mist.

Finally, when all the smoke had left the vessel, it condensed and took the form of a huge, fierce-looking genie who, rearing up in front of the fisherman, roared:

'Aha, so it was you who delivered me. Prepare to die, for I will surely kill you! King Solomon shut me up in that bottle centuries ago, and for a long time I was ready to reward the man who would deliver me, but when he took so long I swore to kill him. Down on your knees and prepare for death!'

In vain the terrified fisherman tried to soften the genie's heart by telling him about his wife and children, but the genie refused to be turned from his purpose. The fisherman was no fool, however. When he saw that he could not soften the evil creature's heart he thought up a stratagem.

'Since I must die,' said he, 'do me the favour of answering just one question, and swear that you will answer it truthfully.'

The genie promised to answer his question, and the fisherman went on:

'When I see how huge you are I cannot believe that you could have been shut up in this bottle.'

'And yet that is where I was!' replied the genie.

'In good faith it does not seem possible. I wish you would show me how you did it, for unless I see it with my own eyes I cannot believe you!'

The genie, angry at having doubt cast on his word after he had sworn to tell the truth, muttered, 'I'll show you!' and as the fisherman watched, the huge body dissolved itself into smoke again and slipped back into the bottle. As soon as the last puff of smoke was safely tucked away, the fisherman seized the cover and swiftly sealed the bottle... and then it was the genie's turn to implore the fisherman to have mercy on him.

Well, there is a lot more to the story, but I have told you this much so that you may understand that such things happen to us also. Every day the entities within you beg to be released, and if you listen to them you will find yourselves in great danger. Before releasing them you should find out all about them, and remember that if they are imprisoned in this way it must be for a good reason. Just as we avoid releasing toxic gases, for instance, in a laboratory, in the same way, we must not release the forces of our subconscious, our instincts and passions. If we release them, it is we who will be the first to suffer. Only the Spirit of God within us should be released.

Freedom is truth expressing itself in the sphere of action. To be free is to act in conformity with divine truth.

By the same author:
(Translated from the French)

Complete Works

Brochures:
New Presentation

Daily Meditations:
A thought for each day of the year.

On the subject of Truth, Wisdom and Love:

Complete Works

VOLUME 1 — THE SECOND BIRTH
Table of contents

To be born a second time is to be born to a new life, the life of the Kingdom of God, the life of the great Universal White Brotherhood.

Two thousand years ago, in Palestine, Jesus gave us the key to all spiritual work when he said, 'Unless a man be born of water and the Spirit, he cannot enter into the Kingdom of God.' Today, the Master Omraam Mikhaël Aïvanhov interprets these words for our benefit. The water Jesus speaks of is Love ; the Spirit, fire, is Wisdom, and Love and Wisdom unite to give birth to Truth which is the new life. In his commentary, the Master Omraam Mikhaël Aïvanhov shows how these three virtues of Love, Wisdom and Truth correspond to man's psychic structure, composed of heart, mind and will. Explaining that our physical bodies mirror our psychic being, he shows how Cosmic Intelligence has inscribed the secret of love in our mouths, that of wisdom in our ears, and that of truth in our eyes.

Editor - Distributor
Editions PROSVETA S.A. — B.P. 12 — 83601 Fréjus Cedex (France)

Distributors
AUSTRIA
  MANDALA
  Verlagsauslieferung für Esoterik
  A-6094 Axams, Innsbruckstraße 7
BELGIUM
  PROSVETA BENELUX
  Van Putlei 105 B-2547 Lint
  N.V. MAKLU Somersstraat 13-15
  B-2018 Antwerpen Tel. (32) 34 55 41 75
  VANDER S.A.
  Av. des Volontaires 321
  B-1150 Bruxelles Tel. (32) 27 62 98 04
BRAZIL
  NOBEL SA
  Rua da Balsa, 559
  CEP 02910 - São Paulo, SP
CANADA
  PROSVETA Inc.
  1565 Montée Masson
  Duvernay est, Laval, Que. H7E 4P2
  Tel. (514) 661-4242   Fax (514) 661-4984
COLUMBIA
  HISAN LTA INGENIEROS
  At/Alvaro MALAVER
  CRA 7 - n°67-02
  Bogotá, Fax 1 212 39 67
CYPRUS
  THE SOLAR CIVILISATION BOOKSHOP
  PO Box 4947, Nicosia
GERMANY
  EDIS GmbH
  Daimlerstr.5
  D - 8029 Sauerlach
GREAT BRITAIN
  PROSVETA
  The Doves Nest
  Duddleswell, Uckfield
  East Sussex TN22 3JJ
GREECE
  PROFIM MARKETING Ltd
  Ifitou 13
  17563 P. Faliro - Athens
HOLLAND
  STICHTING
  PROSVETA NEDERLAND
  Zeestraat 50
  2042 LC Zandvoort
HONG KONG
  SWINDON BOOK CO LTD.
  246 Deck 2, Ocean Terminal
  Harbour City
  Tsimshatsui, Kowloon

IRELAND
  PROSVETA IRL.
  84 Irishtown
  Clonmel
ITALY
  PROSVETA Coop.
  11 via della Resistenza
  06060 Moiano (PG)
LUXEMBOURG
  PROSVETA BENELUX
  Van Putlei 105 B-2548 Lint
MEXICO
  COLOFON S.A.
  Pitagora 1143
  Colonia del Valle
  03 100 Mexico, D.F.
NEW ZEALAND
  Psychic Books
  P.O. Box 87-151
  Meadowbank, Auckland 5
NORWAY
  PROSVETA NORDEN
  Postboks 5101
  1501 Moss
PORTUGAL
  PUBLICAÇÕES
  EUROPA-AMERICA Ltd
  Est Lisboa-Sintra KM 14
  2726 Mem Martins Codex
SPAIN
  ASOCIACIÓN PROSVETA ESPAÑOLA
  C/ Ausias March n° 23 Ático
  SP-08010 Barcelona
SWITZERLAND
  PROSVETA
  Société Coopérative
  CH - 1808 Les Monts-de-Corsier
  Tel. (41) 21 921 92 18
  Fax   (41) 21 923 51 27
UNITED STATES
  PROSVETA U.S.A.
  P.O. Box 49614
  Los Angeles
  California 90049
VENEZUELA
  J.P. Leroy
  Apartado 51 745
  Sabana Grande
  1050 A - Caracas

Printed by
Ateliers Graphiques Marc Veilleux Inc.
Cap-Saint-Ignace, Québec
in June 1994.